THE BALTI SECRETS
OF THE BIRMINGHAM
BALTI COMPANY

THE BALTI SECRETS
OF THE BIRMINGHAM
BALTI COMPANY

JANET AND PETER LARDNER

foulsham
LONDON • NEW YORK • TORONTO • SYDNEY

foulsham

The Publishing House, Bennetts Close,
Cippenham, Slough, Berkshire SL1 5AP

ISBN 0-572-02298-0

Typeset in Great Britain by Typesetting Solutions, Slough, Berks.
Printed in Great Britain by St. Edmundsbury Press, Bury St. Edmunds, Suffolk.

CONTENTS

ABOUT THE AUTHORS

Living in the centre of the Balti belt of Birmingham, it was inevitable that Janet and Peter Lardner would become Balti curry addicts. After many happy and memorable trips to restaurants throughout the area, they decided that the whole Balti experience, with its simple methods of cooking and eating, was a joy not to be missed. Balti should – and could – be made available to many more people. With this plan in mind, they formed the Birmingham Balti Co., offering a comprehensive range of Balti spices and blends, utensils and Balti cookery kits. In addition to its mail order operations, the Birmingham Balti Co. now retails to major high street stores.

Janet has worked in catering for ten years and is now administrator of the Birmingham Balti Co.; Peter runs the company's production and sales, and teaches Balti cookery at local colleges in the region. The couple give regular Balti cookery demonstrations throughout the United Kingdom and Eire.

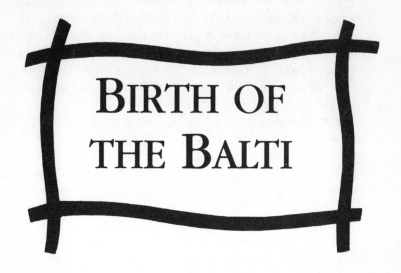

BIRTH OF THE BALTI

Over the centuries, throughout the north-western region of India and Pakistan, nomadic people travelled through the Himalayas from Kashmir and Baltistan to China, trading in silk and spices. On their travels they became influenced by the flavours and textures of the food from the Mogul empire and adapted this form of cooking to their own way of life. The Balti cooking pan was adapted from the Chinese wok. From this, the travellers prepared, cooked and ate from the same dish.

In modern times the 'Balti', as it became known, was served in local roadside cafés to travellers throughout the region. The President of Pakistan heard about the dish and promptly travelled to try the delights of Balti. He was suitably impressed, and the popularity of the Balti began to spread.

More recently, it was the arrival of the Kashmiri people – some fleeing the hostilities in their homeland – that brought the Balti to Britain. The first Balti restaurant opened in Birmingham in the 1970s. The early Balti restaurants offered a selection of simple meat, chicken and fish Baltis, although the customer could request variations such as chicken with mushroom, meat with mixed vegetables, and so on. With changing combinations of spices, today's chefs have been able to create many more exciting Balti dishes. A Balti menu may now offer up to 60 variations.

Balti restaurants still tend to prefer a basic café style, with an easy-going atmosphere. The relaxed ambience carries through with the food, as the Balti is served in a traditional 'karahi' or 'kadoi' and eaten with freshly baked chapati or naan bread. The restaurants offer a selection of starters and sweets. The majority of starters are cooked on an open flame barbecue, with kebab and tikka specialities. The sweets are often milk based with pistachio and cardamom flavouring. Other sweets, such as Kulfi or Jalabis, are also Balti favourites.

There is a popular myth, inspired by the traditional secrecy of chefs, that Balti is difficult to prepare and cook. On the contrary, by virtue of its universal cooking utensil, the Balti is a particularly simple form of cuisine.

We have included in this book a selection of quick and easy recipes. Some are based on the traditional method of Balti cooking while others follow the restaurant style of cooking. Both methods produce delicious, tasty meals in less than an hour.

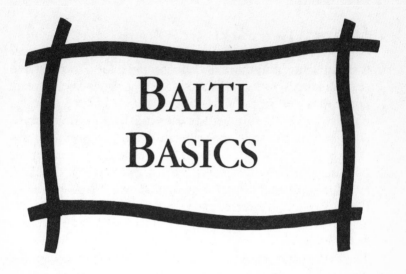

CHAPTER TWO

BALTI BASICS

A traditional Balti is a delicious combination of aromatic spices, onions, tomatoes and lashings of fresh coriander. It is stir fried in a pan similar to a Chinese 'wok', known as a 'karahi'. By mixing these ingredients together, creative Balti chefs realised that they could produce a base sauce which, when cooked with meat, fish or chicken, produced an aromatic, mouth-watering dish in minutes.

In more recent years, Balti chefs have applied their cooking techniques to popular curry-based dishes such as Madras, Dopiaza and Korma – creating what is now known as Balti Madras, Balti Dopiaza, and many other sumptuous Balti combinations.

The beauty of a Balti is that it is a simple, quick and easy dish to prepare. You are free to experiment with spices and combinations of meat, fish and vegetables: in fact, anything left in your cupboard can be used to create a delicious Balti.

Before you start enjoying the Balti recipes in this book, please take a few moments to read through the following basic points.

Enjoying your Balti

Balti is great fun to eat. The food will be 'sizzling' as you carry it to the table, and there is really no need for a formal table setting: knives, forks and spoons are not necessary. In years gone by, travelling nomads cooked Balti in a karahi over hot embers, and the resulting dish was eaten by the whole family, straight from the pan, using unleavened bread. So, when you cook Balti at home, all you need is some delicious naan bread or a chapati. Tear off a piece of the bread, dip it in the Balti, and scoop the food into your mouth. Make sure you have plenty of serviettes or finger bowls available!

Equipment

The Balti cooking pan – the karahi – is a round, two-handled pan which is available in a variety of sizes and metals. A diameter of around 28-30 cm/11-12 inches is ideal for cooking: this would be large enough for four to six portions. Always read the manufacturer's instructions before using the pan.

To serve, you transfer the Balti into smaller, individual dishes with a diameter of around 18-22 cm/7-9 inches, depending on the eater's appetite. This smaller pan, called a 'kadoi', is also suitable for cooking side vegetable dishes.

Chapati and puri (or 'roti') breads are cooked on a 'tawa'. This is a circular, slightly concave, wrought iron disc, which is placed over the heat source. If you do not have a tawa, a heavy shallow frying pan will suffice.

You will also need a bowl for mixing marinades and dough, a chopping board, a variety of spoons – teaspoons, tablespoons, a wooden spoon and a slotted spoon – and a selection of knives. A mortar and pestle will be useful for mixing and grinding spices, and a rolling pin is necessary for rolling the chapati. This rolling pin is a thinner version of the traditional British style of rolling pin. A food processor is handy for mixing and slicing vegetables, and a blender will also save you time and effort.

Spices

Spices are an integral part of the Balti flavour. They should be kept in an air-tight container in a cool, dry, dark place, such as a cupboard in your kitchen.

Traditionally, spices are stored in a 'Masala Dabba', which is a stainless steel container with seven individual pots inside. If there is a particular Balti or curry that you cook frequently, you can store the relevant spices in your Masala Dabba. This will save you rummaging through a cupboard to find the ones that you need.

A good supply of basic herbs and spices will hold you in good stead for the unexpected Balti request: for example, ground coriander, fenugreek leaves, turmeric, ground cumin, ground ginger and chilli.

Cardamom

Two types of cardamom (or 'illachi') are used in Asian cooking. Green cardamoms have a strong, sweet aromatic flavour and are ideal for flavouring sweets, curries and drinks. Black cardamoms are used whole and have a bitter, sour taste.

Coriander

(or 'dhania') is an essential ingredient for Balti cuisine. Ground coriander has a strong earthy flavour, while the seeds have a slight orangy taste. Ground coriander can lose its flavour quickly, so always throw it away once it is out of date.

Cumin

(or 'jeera') is an aromatic, pungent spice, grown throughout the Middle East and India. The seed is used – both whole and ground – for cooking. Cumin is also a main ingredient for Garam Masala.

Chilli

(or 'mirich') can be used fresh, dried or ground. Whole red dried chillies will add colour and are milder in taste than fresh chillies. If you are using fresh chillies but you do not require a 'hot' flavour, then remember to remove the seeds. Whole uncut chillies will also add flavour without the heat.

Turmeric

(or 'haldi') is a bright, orange-yellow colour. Turmeric is used for colouring and flavour. It has a mild aroma with a slightly bitter taste.

Balti Blends

To make Balti cooking even quicker and easier, it is worth having a good supply of the Balti Masala blends at hand (see next section). When creating your own Masala blends, be sure to roast the whole spices either by dry-roasting in the oven or dry-frying until you can smell the aromatic fragrance. This will only take a few minutes. Grind the roasted spices together and store in an airtight container.

Herbs

Fresh coriander, mint and fenugreek are used widely in Balti cooking. They can all be purchased fresh but are generally sold in rather large bunches. To keep your coriander fresh for 5–7 days, place it in a jar of water, cover with a plastic bag and keep in your refrigerator. Change the water every day. Fenugreek and mint can be stored in the refrigerator in the same way.

If you want to freeze these herbs, then separate the bunch, cut off the roots and any yellow leaves, place on an absorbent towel and leave to dry. When dry, place in a plastic bag and freeze for later use.

Incidentally, fenugreek leaves should be cooked whole but without the stalks as they have a bitter taste.

Garlic and Ginger

These will keep fresh if stored in a cool, dry place, away from direct sunlight. When buying fresh ginger, look for the slimmer pieces that feel firm and moist. The thicker, drier ginger is probably old and will contain rather fibrous stems which cannot be used. Quick and easy garlic and ginger pureé recipes are included in the next section of this book.

Dried Herbs and Spices

If you use fresh spices or herbs rather than the dried versions, then use double the amount mentioned in the recipes. For instance, if the recipe says '2 tsp ground coriander', then replace with 4 tsp fresh coriander.

Food Colourings

Red and yellow food colourings are used frequently in Balti cuisine. Natural colourings are recommended: beetroot for red food colouring; and turmeric, saffron or egg yellow for yellow food colouring.

Oils

Always choose a good quality product. Corn oil or sunflower oil is recommended for deep frying. You can also use these oils for cooking Balti curry.

Mustard oil is extracted from brown or black mustard seeds. It has a distinct flavour and is used mainly for Indian pickles. When using mustard oil for general cooking, dilute it with a blander oil. Olive oil should never be used as it imparts a strong flavour and does not lend itself to Balti cooking.

Once opened, these oils should be stored in a dark, cool environment. They should not be refrigerated.

Ghee

This is basically clarified butter. Although it can be purchased in supermarkets and Asian grocery stores, you can make it at home very simply (see next section). To store ghee, keep it in a sealed container and refrigerate. If you are keen on healthy eating, you can buy vegetable ghee at your local supermarket.

Flours

Made from a variety of cereals, pulses and lentils, flour is used for making breads and batter mixes. It is also a useful thickening agent. All the flours mentioned in this book are readily available at Asian grocers and supermarkets.

Gram flour (or 'besan' flour) is made from ground chick peas, and has a distinctive flavour and texture. You can use it for batter mixes and as a thickening agent. Store it in an airtight jar.

Wholemeal flour (or 'atta') is used for making chapatis. It can be purchased as light wholemeal flour or a heavier brown wholemeal flour. Ask for chapati flour when purchasing.

Finally, 'maida' flour is a fine, white flour used for making naan breads. In this book, we have replaced maida flour with plain white flour or self-raising flour.

Meats

For quick and easy Balti cooking, lamb and beef are recommended. Look for fat-free cuts, and always dice the meat into bite-sized pieces, e.g. 2.5 cm/1 inch squares. For beef dishes, you can cut down the cooking time by using the most tender cuts, such as sirloin, topside, rump or fillet. Best quality minced beef tends to be less fatty than cheaper mince. If the mince is fatty, boil it first and leave it to cool. The fat can then be spooned off.

Lamb should be boned and fat free. Leg of lamb is probably the best cut to choose, especially for cooking kebabs. Diced lamb will suffice but there will be more fat and it will take much longer to cook. When purchasing minced lamb, pick your piece of lamb first and then ask the butcher to mince it for you.

Chicken is also used widely in Balti cooking. It is very quick to cook and easily absorbs the flavours of the spices.

Fish and Shellfish

In recent years, fish has become the basis of some very popular Balti meals. Many of the sea water fish and freshwater species available throughout Britain can be used to create delicious and healthy Baltis for the family. Firm white fish varieties are most suitable, such as cod, monk fish, halibut, pollack and hake.

When purchasing fresh fish, look for brightness of eyes and a moist and glossy skin. The scales on the fish should not be damaged. For filleted fish, look for a texture which seems firm and not mushy. Avoid fish which has a blue tinge.

Storing and Freezing

The many spices and tomatoes used in Balti recipes are natural preserving agents. Therefore, once your Balti has cooled, it can be placed in a refrigerator and stored for up to 4–5 days. As soon as you have finished cooking, transfer the Balti from the karahi to a bowl. Allow it to cool, cover with cling film or a cloth, and place in the refrigerator.

Balti is ideally suited for freezing. In fact, the flavours of the spices seem to be enhanced when your favourite Balti dish has been frozen and re-heated. You can keep 'leftovers' frozen for around 2–3 months. Alternatively, you can slightly undercook your favourite Balti dishes, and freeze them for up to 6–8 months.

How should you reheat your frozen Balti? The first step is to thaw it out completely. If the Balti was fully cooked before you froze it, then you simply need to reheat it as follows: heat 1 tbsp of oil or ghee in a karahi over a medium heat. Add the Balti and bring it to the boil before reducing the heat and simmering for 5–8 minutes, stirring continuously. If you have frozen a par-cooked Balti dish, then follow the same procedure, but simmer for 15 minutes, stirring occasionally.

To reheat a fully-cooked Balti using a microwave, place the defrosted Balti in a covered dish and microwave it on full power for 1–2 minutes. To serve, simply warm a kadoi and pour in the cooked Balti.

Time-saving Tips

A little forward preparation will help a busy Balti chef when he/she is planning to cook a Balti meal. When you start to cook from a recipe, try to prepare all the ingredients first and have everything to hand. This will save a lot of time when you start cooking. Always keep a good supply of the basic Balti spices and blends to hand, and always freeze the remainder of your fresh coriander, mint and fenugreek.

Pre-prepared base sauces, meats and pureés can reduce the cooking time by more than half. Note that dried onion flakes can be used to replace fresh onions when preparing the base Balti sauces. Par-boiling potatoes will save time when cooking a vegetable Balti. Always choose a firm, waxy potato.

Pastry for samosa starters can be frozen and used at a later date. You can also prepare the meat filling at an earlier point and then freeze it.

There are a number of ready-made naan breads and popadoms available on the market today, which are ideal for the time-conscious chef.

Balti Heat

We all have varying tastes and preferences. This can some-times create problems for the home Balti chef, especially if some members of the family prefer their Balti to be hotter or milder than the others. It is simple to overcome this problem.

If you are a 'heat fanatic', then follow these steps. When the main Balti is three-quarters cooked, heat a little oil or ghee in a separate karahi. Add to this a portion of the main Balti, plus one or two chopped, fresh chillies, and bring to the boil. Then simmer for the remainder of the cooking time.

For a milder Balti, transfer a portion of the fully-cooked main Balti dish to another karahi. Add two tablespoons of natural yoghurt, stir in and cook gently for 1–2 minutes.

CHAPTER THREE

PREPARING FOR ACTION

An excellent way to speed up your Balti cooking is to make the necessary blends, sauces, purées and ghee in advance and then store or refrigerate them. You can also par-cook your meats and then freeze them ready for future use. The following recipes will help you prepare for action!

TANDOORI MASALA

This Masala mix will give your Tikka and Tandoori dishes flavour and colouring.

MAKES 75 g / 3 oz

INGREDIENTS	METRIC	IMPERIAL	AMERICAN
WHOLE SPICES			
White cumin seeds	30 ml	½ oz	2 tbsp
White peppercorns	30 ml	½ oz	2 tbsp
Black cardamom seeds	2.5 ml	½ tsp	½ tsp
Cassia bark	5 cm	2 in	2 in
Whole cloves	8	8	8
GROUND SPICES			
Saffron, 4-5 strands	4-5	4-5	4-5
Ground cumin	30 ml	½ oz	2 tbsp
Ground mace	7.5 ml	1½ tsp	1½ tsp
Ground nutmeg	2.5 ml	½ tsp	½ tsp
Red food colouring (optional)	10 ml	2 tsp	2 tsp

1 Mix all the spices together in small quantities and grind them until fine.

2 Store in an airtight container in a dark, dry place.

BALTI MASALA

T his is used as a base spice blend to give your Balti cuisine the authentic Balti flavour.

MAKES 175 g / 6 oz

INGREDIENTS	METRIC	IMPERIAL	AMERICAN
WHOLE SPICES			
Coriander seeds	75 ml	5 tbsp	5 tbsp
White cumin seeds	30 ml	2 tbsp	2 tbsp
Fennel seeds	10 ml	2 tsp	2 tsp
Black mustard seeds	10 ml	2 tsp	2 tsp
Fenugreek seeds	5 ml	1 tsp	1 tsp
Whole cloves	4-5	4-5	4-5
Bay leaves	4	4	4
Curry leaves	25 g	1 oz	¼ cup
Lovage seeds	5 ml	1 tsp	1 tsp
Onion seeds	2.5 ml	½ tsp	½ tsp
Cassia bark	3 x 5 cm	3 x 2 in	3 x 2 in
Fenugreek leaves	15 ml	1 tbsp	1 tbsp
GROUND SPICES			
Chilli powder	7.5 ml	1½ tsp	1½ tsp
Ground ginger	10 ml	2 tsp	2 tsp
Ground cardamom	5 ml	1 tsp	1 tsp
Garlic powder	15 ml	1 tbsp	1 tbsp
Turmeric	15 ml	1 tbsp	1 tbsp

1 Roast all the whole spices by placing them in a non-stick roasting pan in a low oven for a 1–2 minutes.

2 When cooled, grind the spice mixture using a food processor or blender.

3 Add the remaining ground spices and mix well.

4 Store in a sealed container or spice jar in a cool, dry, dark place.

BALTI GARAM MASALA

T his Balti Garam Masala differs from the Garam Masala used in other Asian dishes because the emphasis is on the aromatic qualities rather than the heat. Balti Garam Masala is added to the food towards the end of the cooking time. It will enhance the dish with that extra flavour for which the Balti is now famous.

MAKES 175 g / 6 oz

INGREDIENTS	METRIC	IMPERIAL	AMERICAN
WHOLE SPICES			
Coriander seeds	75 ml	5 tbsp	5 tbsp
White cumin seeds	40 ml	2½ tbsp	2½ tbsp
Cassia bark	5 x 5 cm	5 x 2 in	5 x 2 in
Mint leaves, dried	7.5 ml	1½ tsp	1½ tsp
Bay leaves	5	5	5
GROUND SPICES			
Ground aniseed	25 ml	5 tsp	5 tsp
Ground cardamom	13 ml	2½ tsp	2½ tsp
Ground cloves	10 ml	2 tsp	2 tsp
Turmeric	5 ml	1 tsp	1 tsp
Paprika	5 ml	1 tsp	1 tsp

1 Lightly roast all the whole spices by placing them in a non-stick roasting pan in a low oven for 1–2 minutes. Leave to cool.

2 Place into a food processor or blender and grind.

3 Add the ground spices and blend well.

4 Store in a spice jar.

GHEE

Ghee is simple to make. It can be stored in an air-tight container for up to two months. For a healthy alternative, you can buy vegetable ghee from your local supermarket.

MAKES 750 g / 1½ lb

INGREDIENTS	METRIC	IMPERIAL	AMERICAN
Butter	900 g	2 lb	4 cups

1. Place the butter in a heavy-based saucepan.

2. Melt it over a low heat, ensuring that it does not smoke or burn.

3. Remove residue from the top and you will be left with a clear liquid.

4. Allow to cool.

BALTI SAUCE

M *any of the recipes included in this book feature Balti base sauces. Although these sauces are not essential in the cooking of Balti, they will save a lot of time and effort when you actually start to cook a Balti.*

The sauces can be frozen or kept refrigerated for 4–5 days. To make extra sauce for freezing, double or treble the quantities below. Separate the sauce into 450 ml/¾ pint portions before freezing.

SERVES 4

INGREDIENTS	METRIC	IMPERIAL	AMERICAN
Onions, peeled and quartered	450 g	1 lb	1 lb
Fresh ginger, peeled and roughly chopped	25 g	1 oz	¼ cup
Garlic cloves, roughly chopped	6	6	6
Salt	to taste	to taste	to taste
Water	450 ml	¾ pt	2 cups
Can tomatoes, chopped	100 g	4 oz	½ cup
Vegetable oil	60 ml	4 tbsp	4 tbsp
Fenugreek leaves, dried	20 ml	4 tsp	4 tsp
Ground black pepper	2.5 ml	½ tsp	½ tsp
Whole green cardamoms, top pinched	4	4	4
Balti Masala	30 ml	2 tbsp	2 tbsp

1 Mix together the water, onions, garlic, ginger and salt in a karahi. Bring to the boil and simmer for 10–15 minutes.

2 Meanwhile, heat the oil in a frying pan, and fry all the spices together. Add the tinned tomatoes and simmer for 10 minutes.

3 When the onion mixture is cooked, stir in the tomato mixture and simmer together for a further 10 minutes.

4 Place the sauce in a blender and blend. It is now ready for use.

Cooking time 20–25 minutes.

MASALA SAUCE

T his smooth, creamy sauce is ideal for cooking Tikka Masala Balti dishes. If you plan to freeze Masala sauce, do not add the fresh coriander. Separate the sauce into 450 ml/¾ pint portions before freezing.

SERVES 4–6

INGREDIENTS	METRIC	IMPERIAL	AMERICAN
Butter	75 g	3 oz	⅓ cup
Vegetable oil	15 ml	1 tbsp	1 tbsp
Onions, finely chopped	175 g	6 oz	6 oz
Fresh tomatoes	450 g	1 lb	1 lb
Single cream	120 ml	4 fl oz	½ cup
Natural yoghurt	30 ml	2 tbsp	2 tbsp
Salt	to taste	to taste	to taste
Chilli powder	5 ml	1 tsp	1 tsp
Whole cumin seeds	15 ml	1 tbsp	1 tbsp
Cassia bark	2.5 cm	1 in	1 in
Fresh coriander	60 ml	4 tbsp	4 tbsp

1 Heat the butter and oil together in a karahi, and gently fry the onions until translucent.

2 Add the spices and tomatoes, and cook for 5–6 minutes or until the oil separates.

3 Pour in the cream and yoghurt, and mix well.

4 Simmer for 3–4 minutes to thicken the sauce.

5 Sprinkle with the fresh coriander.

Cooking time 10–15 minutes.

GINGER PURÉE

*R*eady-made ginger purée can be purchased from your local supermarket, but it can be expensive. It is simple to make yourself and will save time in preparation.

If you store ginger purée in a refrigerator, it can stay fresh for up to 10 days. Alternatively, it can be frozen in plastic bags or in an ice cube tray. The cubes can be used as required.

MAKES 225 g / 8 oz

INGREDIENTS	METRIC	IMPERIAL	AMERICAN
Fresh ginger	225 g	8 oz	8 oz
Vegetable oil	30 ml	2 tbsp	2 tbsp
Water	5 ml	1 tsp	1 tsp

1 Using a potato peeler, peel the ginger.

2 Chop it roughly against the grain.

3 Place it in a blender, add the oil and water and blend to a fine paste. If you are using a food processor, process to a smooth, fine paste without adding water or oil.

4 Transfer to a jar or container and seal.

GARLIC PURÉE

Since garlic purée can be expensive to buy, you might prefer to make your own.

MAKES 225 g / 8 oz

INGREDIENTS	METRIC	IMPERIAL	AMERICAN
Garlic cloves, peeled	225g	8 oz	8 oz
Vegetable oil	30 ml	2 tbsp	2 tbsp

1. Place the garlic cloves and oil into a blender and process to a smooth, fine paste.

2. Transfer to an air tight jar and store in the salad drawer of your refrigerator.

PAR-COOKED MEAT

*M*eat tends to take a little longer than poultry to cook thoroughly. So, if time is of the essence, you should par-cook your meat in advance and split it into portions for freezing. You will then have a ready supply of par-cooked meats available for use. If you are planning to stock your freezer with par-cooked meat, double or treble the amounts listed in this recipe.

SERVES 4

INGREDIENTS	METRIC	IMPERIAL	AMERICAN
Lamb or beef, off the bone	450 g	1 lb	1 lb
Onion, roughly chopped	1	1	1
Fresh ginger, chopped and peeled	25 g	1 oz	¼ cup
Garlic cloves, chopped	3	3	3
Salt	2.5 ml	½ tsp	½ tsp
Balti Masala	7.5 ml	1½ tsp	1½ tsp
Water	300 ml	½ pt	1¼ cups

1. Trim any fat off the meat and cut into bite-sized pieces.

2. Place all the ingredients in a saucepan.

3. Bring to the boil and cover with a lid.

4. Simmer for 30–35 minutes.

5. Drain away the stock. This can be strained and used later as curry stock.

6. When cooled, split the meat into portions and freeze.

Cooking time 35–40 minutes.

PAR-COOKED CHICKEN

A n easy way to reduce cooking time is to par-cook your chicken before use.

SERVES 4

INGREDIENTS	METRIC	IMPERIAL	AMERICAN
Chicken, boned and skinned	750 g	1½ lb	1½ lb
Onion, peeled and chopped	1	1	1
Ghee	40 g	1½ oz	3 tbsp
Balti Masala	5 ml	1 tsp	1 tsp
Salt	to taste	to taste	to taste
Water	600 ml	1 pt	2½ cups

1   Cut the chicken into bite-sized pieces.

2   Place all the ingredients in a saucepan.

3   Bring to the boil.

4   Cover pan with a lid and simmer for 20 minutes.

5   Drain away stock.

6   When cooled, split into portions and freeze or cook in your Balti dish.

Cooking time 25 minutes.

SNACKS & STARTERS

Balti addicts will recognise many of the recipes here from Balti restaurant menus. The dishes can be served as appetising starters or as snack meals.

Some of the dishes, such as Chicken Tikka and Tandoori Fish, are best cooked after the meat has been marinated for 3–5 hours. To save time, prepare the marinade the day before and leave the meat to soak overnight. Cooking will then be extremely quick and easy.

POPADOMS

A popadom is a crisp flat bread made from a mixture of rice and lentil flour. The dough mix is rolled wafer thin and sun dried. It is then stored until cooked. When eaten with a crunchy fresh chutney and raita, popadoms make an excellent starter.

However, popadoms can be quite difficult to make, so we would recommend that busy cooks buy the ready-made variety. They are available in a number of flavours, including garlic, cumin, pepper, red chilli and, of course, plain. Since packets of popadoms tend to lack any cooking instructions, we have listed some methods below.

Grilling

1. Place popadom under the grill.

2. When it is a light golden colour all over and small bubbles appear, take it away from the heat. The popadom will feel soft and pliable at this stage. Do not burn!

3. Leave to cool.

Frying

1. Heat 30–45 ml/2–3 tbsp vegetable oil in a frying pan.

2. Add the popadom and cook for 1 minute. The popadom will bubble and fluff.

3. Take it out of the oil. Stand the popadom on its end to drain.

Microwave

1. Microwave at high heat for 1–2 minutes.

PRAWN PURI

Jhinga Puri

*I*n this delicious dish, the prawns are cooked in a Masala sauce and served on a freshly cooked puri (see the Breads section).

SERVES 4

INGREDIENTS	METRIC	IMPERIAL	AMERICAN
Frozen prawns, defrosted	225 g	8 oz	8 oz
Masala sauce	200 ml	7 fl oz	1 cup
Coconut powder	10 ml	2 tsp	2 tsp
Almonds, ground	5 ml	1 tsp	1 tsp
Freshly cooked puri	4	4	4
FOR THE GARNISH			
Fresh coriander	15 ml	1 tbsp	1 tbsp

1. Heat the Masala sauce gently in a karahi until it is simmering.

2. Stir in the coconut powder and prawns, and cook for 3–5 minutes.

3. Mix in the ground almonds and take the karahi away from the heat.

4. Place four puris on a plate, and spoon a quarter of the sauce on top of each.

5. Garnish with fresh coriander.

Preparation time 5 minutes.

Cooking time 10 minutes.

VEGETABLE PAKORA

T *his recipe is for Potato Pakora, but you can replace the potato with any number of vegetables such as broccoli florets, spinach, cauliflower florets, mushrooms and aubergines (eggplants). Alternatively you can combine a selection of different vegetables to make Mixed Pakora.*

Pakora will stay fresh for 4–5 days if stored in a covered dish in the refrigerator. They can also be frozen.

SERVES 4

INGREDIENTS	METRIC	IMPERIAL	AMERICAN
Potatoes, peeled and finely sliced	350 g	12 oz	12 oz
FOR BATTER MIX			
Gram flour	175 g	6 oz	1½ cups
Garlic cloves, crushed	2	2	2
Chilli powder	5 ml	1 tsp	1 tsp
Balti Masala	4 ml	¾ tsp	¾ tsp
Fenugreek leaves	5 ml	1 tsp	1 tsp
Salt	to taste	to taste	to taste
Water	175 ml	6 fl oz	¾ cup
Vegetable oil	600 ml	1 pt	2½ cups

1 Sift the gram flour into a bowl.

2 Gradually add the water to make a smooth batter.

3 Add all the ingredients, except the oil, and mix well.

4 Heat the vegetable oil in a karahi, wok or deep frying pan to a high temperature, then turn down the heat.

⑤ Drop a tablespoonful of the batter into the hot oil and allow it to sizzle.

⑥ If the oil is sufficiently hot, the batter will drop to the bottom of the pan. It will then immediately rise to the surface and float.

⑦ Fry several batches of eight or nine pakora at a time, turning them over frequently so that they become golden brown all over.

⑧ Lift them out of the oil with a slotted spoon and drain on absorbent paper.

SERVING SUGGESTION

Serve with a green salad and tamarind and onion chutney or mint raita.

Preparation time 7–8 minutes.

Cooking time 5–10 minutes.

CHICKEN PAKORA

*Chicken Pakora can make an excellent starter dish.
If you are having a dinner party, you can offer your
guests a combination of flavours and textures by serving both Vegetable and Chicken Pakora. You can freeze
the Pakora immediately after cooling.*

SERVES 4

INGREDIENTS	METRIC	IMPERIAL	AMERICAN
Cooked chicken, cubed	350 g	12 oz	12 oz
FOR BATTER MIX			
Gram flour	175 g	6 oz	1½ cups
Water	120 ml	4 fl oz	½ cup
Garlic cloves, crushed	2	2	2
Chilli powder	5 ml	1 tsp	1 tsp
Balti Masala	2.5 ml	½ tsp	½ tsp
Soy sauce	10 ml	2 tsp	2 tsp
Fenugreek leaves	5 ml	1 tsp	1 tsp
White cumin seeds	5 ml	1 tsp	1 tsp
Salt	to taste	to taste	to taste
Vegetable oil	600 ml	1 pt	2½ cups

1. Heat the oil in a karahi, wok or deep frying pan.

2. Sift the gram flour into a bowl and gradually add the water to make a smooth paste.

3. Add all the remaining ingredients and mix well.

4. Using a spoon, place one coated chicken piece at a time into the hot oil.

⑤ Fry both sides of the pakora until golden brown.

⑥ Take out with a slotted spoon and allow to drain.

Preparation time 6 minutes.

Cooking time 15 minutes.

FISH PAKORA

*R*eplace the cooked chicken with 450 g/1 lb of uncooked fish. Choose a firm white fish and cut into cubes.

SEEKH KEBABS

*M*any people are familiar with the large charcoal *grill, usually situated at the entrance of a traditional Balti restaurant. It is here that the kebabs and tikkas are cooked. Do not dismay! The recipes are also well suited to home cooking. Remember, when the summer arrives, these dishes are ideal for cooking on your barbecue.*

If possible, the meat and spices should be left to marinate for up to an hour prior to cooking.

SERVES 4-6

INGREDIENTS	METRIC	IMPERIAL	AMERICAN
Minced lamb	450 g	1 lb	1 lb
Gram flour	30 ml	2 tbsp	2 tbsp
Onion, finely chopped	100 g	4 oz	1 cup
Garlic cloves, crushed	2	2	2
Ground coriander	5 ml	1 tsp	1 tsp
Chilli powder	5 ml	1 tsp	1 tsp
White cumin seeds	2.5 ml	½ tsp	½ tsp
Fresh green chillies, finely chopped	2	2	2
Balti Masala	2.5 ml	½ tsp	½ tsp
Salt	to taste	to taste	to taste
Fresh coriander leaves, chopped	15 ml	1 tbsp	1 tbsp
Lemon juice	5 ml	1 tsp	1 tsp

❶ In a bowl, mix all the ingredients together.

❷ Knead the mixture for 5 minutes to form a paste-like consistency. If possible, leave to marinate for an hour.

❸ Divide the mixture into around ten equal parts, each made into a ball.

④ With a skewer, press through the centre of a ball. Moisten your hands with water or a little oil, and press the mince paste into a sausage shape 8–10 cm/3–4 inches long. If you are using lean meat, brush the kebabs lightly with oil or melted ghee.

⑤ Place the kebab under the grill at a low heat for 5–10 minutes. When barbecuing, turn the kebabs constantly.

⑥ Increase the heat briefly to brown the kebabs.

Preparation time 10 minutes.

Standing time 1 hour (optional).

Cooking time 7–10 minutes.

SHAMI KEBABS

A *Shami is a flat, burger-like kebab, popular in Balti*
restaurants. If stored in a cool place, Shami Kebabs
will stay fresh for 4-5 days. They can also be frozen.

SERVES 4-6

INGREDIENTS	METRIC	IMPERIAL	AMERICAN
Lamb, finely minced	450 g	1 lb	1 lb
Fresh green chillies	4	4	4
Garlic cloves	6	6	6
Onion, finely chopped	100 g	4 oz	1 cup
Fresh ginger, finely chopped	15 g	½ oz	2 tbsp
Fresh tomato, finely chopped	1	1	1
Lemon juice	5 ml	1 tsp	1 tsp
Chilli powder	2.5 ml	½ tsp	½ tsp
Salt	to taste	to taste	to taste
Gram flour	10 ml	2 tsp	2 tsp
Egg	1	1	1
Vegetable oil	30 ml	2 tbsp	2 tbsp
Fresh coriander leaves	15 ml	1 tbsp	1 tbsp

1 Mix together the above ingredients, except the fresh
   coriander leaves, lemon juice, oil, egg and gram flour.

2 Place the mixture in a deep frying pan, cover with
   water and bring to the boil. Do not cover.

3 Simmer the mixture until the water has evaporated
   and the mixture is dry.

4 Cool the mixture. Make sure it is dry before moving
   on to the next step.

⑤ Use a blender to blend the mixture to a fine paste. Add the egg, lemon juice, gram flour and coriander leaves, and mix together.

⑥ Divide into ten equal parts and mould into burger-like shapes.

⑦ Heat the oil in the frying pan, then fry the kebabs until golden brown.

⑧ Drain on an absorbent cloth.

SERVING SUGGESTION

Serve with a green salad and fresh lime.

Preparation time 10 minutes.

Cooking time 7–10 minutes.

FISH KEBABS

*T*hese are similar to our home-grown fish cakes. With the addition of herbs and spices, Fish Kebabs make an interesting and tasty starter.

SERVES 4

INGREDIENTS	METRIC	IMPERIAL	AMERICAN
FOR KEBABS			
Cooked white fish, skinned and boned	450 g	1 lb	1 lb
Can tomatoes, strained	100 g	4 oz	½ cup
Balti Masala	10 ml	2 tsp	2 tsp
Chilli powder	5 ml	1 tsp	1 tsp
Cumin seeds	2.5 ml	½ tsp	½ tsp
Fresh coriander leaves, chopped	15 ml	1 tbsp	1 tbsp
Lemon juice	10 ml	2 tsp	2 tsp
Salt	to taste	to taste	to taste
FOR COOKING			
Gram flour	100 g	4 oz	1 cup
Egg, beaten	1	1	1
Ghee	50 g	2 oz	¼ cup

❶ Chop and then crush the fish. Blend it with the other kebab ingredients.

❷ Shape the fish mixture into small round cakes around 7 cm/3 inches diameter, 0.75 cm/¼ inch thick.

❸ Dip the fish cakes into the egg, then the gram flour.

④ Shallow fry them in the ghee until golden brown.

SERVING SUGGESTION

Serve with lemon wedges and raita.

Preparation time 5 minutes.

Cooking time 3–5 minutes.

SPICED LAMB CHOPS

Barrah Kebabs

These tender lamb chops are marinated with tantalising spices and then simply grilled.

SERVES 4

INGREDIENTS	METRIC	IMPERIAL	AMERICAN
Small lamb chops, chump or shoulder	8	8	8
Yoghurt	85 g	3 fl oz	5½ tbsp
Malt vinegar, light	30 ml	2 tbsp	2 tbsp
Fresh ginger, chopped	25 g	1 oz	¼ cup
Garlic cloves	6	6	6
Onion, finely chopped	50 g	2 oz	½ cup
Balti Masala	10 ml	2 tsp	2 tsp
Tandoori Masala	5 ml	1 tsp	1 tsp
Mint leaves, dried	5 ml	1 tsp	1 tsp
Fresh coriander, including stalks, chopped	15 g	½ oz	2 tbsp
Salt	5 ml	1 tsp	1 tsp
Vegetable oil	45 ml	3 tbsp	3 tbsp
FOR THE GARNISH			
Balti Garam Masala	2.5 ml	½ tsp	½ tsp
Lemon, cut into wedges	1	1	1
Lettuce	1	1	1
Cucumber	½	½	½

❶ Place the lamb chops in a shallow dish.

❷ Blend all the remaining ingredients together, except the oil.

③ Pour the mixture over the lamb chops, making sure that the chops are completely covered. Place in a refrigerator and marinate for 4–6 hours or overnight.

④ Pre-heat the grill to a medium heat. Place the chops in a lined grill pan, and brush with oil.

⑤ Grill for 3–4 minutes. Turn the chops and baste with oil and juices. Grill for a further 3–4 minutes.

⑥ Transfer to a serving dish. Sprinkle the Balti Garam Masala over the chops and garnish with lemon, lettuce and cucumber.

Preparation time 10 minutes.

Marinating time 4–6 hours.

Cooking time 8 minutes.

CHICKEN TIKKA

Murgh Tikka

This dish consists of succulent pieces of marinated chicken. The chicken should be marinated for around 5 hours or overnight. To save time in the future, you can cook extra Chicken Tikka and then freeze it for a later occasion.

SERVES 6

INGREDIENTS	METRIC	IMPERIAL	AMERICAN
Chicken, boned, skinned and cubed	900 g	2 lb	2 lb
Ghee	15 ml	1 tbsp	1 tbsp
FOR THE MARINADE			
Natural yoghurt	120 ml	4 fl oz	½ cup
Tandoori Masala	5 ml	1 tsp	1 tsp
Lemon juice	10 ml	2 tsp	2 tsp
Salt	to taste	to taste	to taste
Chilli powder	5 ml	1 tsp	1 tsp
Fresh ginger, grated	15 ml	3 tsp	3 tsp
Fresh green chillies	2	2	2
Bay leaf	1	1	1
Whole green cardamoms	3	3	3
FOR THE GARNISH			
Lemon, cut into wedges	1	1	1
Small onion, cut into rings	1	1	1

① Mix together all the marinade ingredients to make a smooth paste.

② Place the chicken in a shallow dish and pour over the marinade paste to cover the chicken pieces.

③ Cover the dish and leave in a cool place overnight or for around 5 hours.

④ Pre-heat the oven to 190°C/375°F/gas mark 5.

⑤ Line a roasting pan with kitchen foil. Take the individual pieces of chicken, shake off excess yoghurt marinade and brush with melted ghee.

⑥ Place the chicken in the roasting pan and cover with foil.

⑦ Place in the oven for 15 minutes.

SERVING SUGGESTION

Garnish with lemon wedges and onion rings. Serve with green salad and chutney.

Preparation time 5 minutes.

Marinating time 5 hours or overnight.

Cooking time 15 minutes.

LAMB TIKKA

Gosht Tikka

*L*amb Tikka comprises tender pieces of lamb, marinated in yoghurt and spices, and is ideal for summer barbecues. It is suitable for freezing.

SERVES 4

INGREDIENTS	METRIC	IMPERIAL	AMERICAN
Lamb, trimmed and cubed	900 g	2 lb	2 lb
FOR THE MARINADE			
Natural yoghurt	120 ml	4 fl oz	½ cup
Fresh green chillies, chopped	4	4	4
Tomato purée	15 ml	1 tbsp	1 tbsp
Garlic purée	7.5 ml	1½ tsp	1½ tsp
Ginger purée	5 ml	1 tsp	1 tsp
Balti Masala	10 ml	2 tsp	2 tsp
Fresh coriander leaves, chopped	15 ml	1 tbsp	1 tbsp
Lemon juice	10 ml	2 tsp	2 tsp
Vegetable oil	15 ml	1 tbsp	1 tbsp
FOR THE GARNISH			
Lemon, cut into wedges	1	1	1
Sprig of fresh coriander	1	1	1

1 In a bowl, mix together all the marinade ingredients.

2 Add the lamb pieces and stir well. Cover and leave in a cool place for 5 hours or overnight.

3 Pre-heat the oven to 220°C/425°F/gas mark 7.

4 Cover a baking tray with kitchen foil.

⑤   Place the lamb pieces on the covered baking tray.

⑥   Cook for 20 minutes on the middle shelf of the oven.

SERVING SUGGESTION

Serve garnished with lemon wedges and fresh coriander.

Preparation 5 minutes.

Standing time 5 hours or overnight.

Cooking time 20 minutes.

NOTE:

If you are cooking Lamb Tikka on a barbecue, place 5-6 lamb pieces on a skewer after marinating. Brush lightly with vegetable oil, then place on the barbecue. Cook for 15 minutes, turning frequently.

TANDOORI CHICKEN

Murgh Tandoor

*T*o make Tandoori Chicken, the whole chicken is marinated with exotic spices and yoghurt, and then traditionally cooked in a tandoor oven. Once cooled, Tandoori Chicken can be frozen for future use.

SERVES 4

INGREDIENTS	METRIC	IMPERIAL	AMERICAN
Whole chicken, skinned and quartered	1.5 kg	3 lb	3 lb
FOR THE MARINADE			
Vegetable oil	50 ml	2 fl oz	3½ tbsp
Fresh green chillies	2	2	2
Whole green cardamoms	2	2	2
Natural yoghurt	120 ml	4 fl oz	½ cup
Fresh ginger, crushed	15 ml	1 tbsp	1 tbsp
Fresh garlic, crushed	15 ml	1 tbsp	1 tbsp
Mango powder (optional)	4 ml	¾ tsp	¾ tsp
Lemon juice	10 ml	2 tsp	2 tsp
Red food colouring (optional)	5 ml	1 tsp	1 tsp
Chilli powder	2.5 ml	½ tsp	½ tsp
Black pepper, freshly ground	5 ml	1 tsp	1 tsp
Salt	5 ml	1 tsp	1 tsp

1 Place the yoghurt in a bowl. Add all the ingredients except the chicken. Mix to form a smooth marinade paste.

2 Cover the chicken with the marinade, rubbing it in to make sure the chicken is well covered. Cover with a cloth or cling film and refrigerate overnight.

(3) Heat the oven to 220°C/425°F/gas mark 7.

(4) Place the chicken on a wire rack in a roasting pan and bake for 15 minutes.

(5) Turn the chicken over and cook for a further 15 minutes.

SERVING SUGGESTION

Garnish with lemon wedges and fresh coriander.

Preparation time 10 minutes.

Marinating time 5 hours or overnight.

Cooking time 30 minutes.

TANDOORI FISH

This is a delicious variation of the tandoori marinated selection. Choose a tasty firm fish such as cod, monkfish, hake or haddock. If you are feeling adventurous, try a tropical fish variety such as snapper.

SERVES 4

INGREDIENTS	METRIC	IMPERIAL	AMERICAN
White fish, skinned	900 g	2 lb	2 lb
FOR THE MARINADE			
Natural yoghurt	120 ml	4 fl oz	½ cup
Whole green cardamoms	2	2	2
Green chillies	4	4	4
Garlic cloves	3	3	3
Tomato purée	10 ml	2 tsp	2 tsp
Lemon juice	10 ml	2 tsp	2 tsp
Chilli powder	5 ml	1 tsp	1 tsp
Black pepper, coarsely ground	2.5 ml	½ tsp	½ tsp
Salt	to taste	to taste	to taste

1   Cut the fish into bite-sized pieces.

2   Blend the fresh chillies, garlic, tomato purée, cardamoms and pepper together to make a fine paste.

3   Pour the yoghurt into a bowl, add the paste and remaining spices, salt and lemon juice. Mix well.

4   Add the fish pieces to the marinade, ensuring that the fish is well covered. Leave to marinate for 2–3 hours.

⑤ Heat the oven to 220°C/425°F/gas mark 7. Place the individual fish pieces on a baking tray in the centre of the oven and bake for 10 minutes.

SERVING SUGGESTION

Serve with mint raita, lemon wedges and green salad.

Preparation time 5 minutes.

Marinating time 2–3 hours.

Cooking time 10 minutes.

MEAT SAMOSA

*D*eep-fried triangular pastries, filled with spiced potatoes and vegetables or meat, are a popular snack throughout India and Pakistan. They are now available in Britain, ready-made, from supermarkets. As ever, for authentic flavour and texture, home-cooked samosas are the superior option. Served as a starter with creamy mint yoghurt or tart tamarind and onion chutney, they are delicious. Samosas can be frozen and reheated at a later date.

MAKES 15

INGREDIENTS	METRIC	IMPERIAL	AMERICAN
FOR THE PASTRY			
Filo pastry, defrosted	225 g	8 oz	8 oz
FOR THE FILLING			
Minced beef or lamb	225 g	8 oz	8 oz
Vegetable oil	30 ml	2 tbsp	2 tbsp
Onion	175 g	6 oz	6 oz
Garlic cloves	2-3	2-3	2-3
Fresh ginger	2.5 cm	1 in	1 in
Lemon juice	5 ml	1 tsp	1 tsp
Cooked peas	175 g	6 oz	1½ cups
Balti Garam Masala	10 ml	2 tsp	2 tsp
Turmeric	2.5 ml	½ tsp	½ tsp
Chilli powder	5 ml	1 tsp	1 tsp
Fresh coriander, chopped	15 ml	1 tbsp	1 tbsp
Salt	to taste	to taste	to taste
Deep frying oil	350 ml	12 fl oz	1½ cups

1. Mince together the onions, garlic and ginger.

2. Fry the meat gently in 2 tbsp oil until brown. Add the minced onion, garlic and ginger. Fry for a further 2 minutes.

3. Stir in the Balti Garam Masala, turmeric and chilli. Flavour with a squeeze of lemon juice and a sprinkle of salt.

4. Add the chopped coriander and cooked peas and stir. Leave to cool.

5. Roll the pastry thinly. Cut it into 20 cm/8 inch circles, then cut these in half.

6. Place the filling in the centre, and pinch the edges together to make a triangular pastry. Make sure that the samosas are well sealed.

7. Deep fry until golden. Drain well.

SERVING SUGGESTION

Serve hot with mint and yoghurt raita or tamarind and onion chutney.

Preparation time 8 minutes.

Cooking time 20 minutes.

VEGETABLE SAMOSAS

Replace the meat with the same weight of diced, cooked potatoes or a combination of potato and cauliflower florets.

ONION BHAJIS

Onion Bhajis are always a firm favourite for a starter.

SERVES 4

INGREDIENTS	METRIC	IMPERIAL	AMERICAN
Large onions, cut into rings	2	2	2
FOR THE BATTER			
Gram flour	75 g	3 oz	¾ cup
Water	85 ml	3 fl oz	5½ tbsp
Chilli powder	5 ml	1 tsp	1 tsp
Ground ginger	5 ml	1 tsp	1 tsp
Balti Masala	2.5 ml	½ tsp	½ tsp
Turmeric	2.5 ml	½ tsp	½ tsp
Vegetable oil	600 ml	1 pt	2½ cups

1. Heat the oil in a karahi, wok or deep frying pan.

2. Sift the gram flour and add the spices. Mix well. Gradually add the water and mix to a smooth paste.

3. Add the onion rings and mix well.

4. Place one coated onion ring at a time in the hot oil. Fry, turning once, until golden brown.

5. When cooked, drain well.

SERVING SUGGESTION

Serve with mint raita and popadoms.

Preparation time 5 minutes.

Cooking time 5–10 minutes.

NOTE:

If you prefer your Bhajis to be a ball shape, chop the onion roughly and mix well in the batter. Take a spoonful of mixture and fry till golden brown.

CHAPTER FIVE

MEAT & POULTRY

In this selection of Balti main dishes, we have included a variety of traditional and restaurant-style recipes for your enjoyment. Remember that Balti is fun to cook: you are free to experiment with the basic recipes by adding your favourite spices, perhaps, or by combining meats, vegetables, pulses and poultry. The world's greatest recipes have been created by experimentation.

CHICKEN BALTI

Murgh Balti

If you have not cooked a Balti meal before, Chicken Balti is a good starting point. Using this simple recipe, you can start to experiment by adding extra ingredients such as mushrooms, peppers and mixed vegetables. Do not worry about authenticity at this stage: the great joy of Balti cuisine is that it has no set rules.

If you wish to save time in the future, why not cook extra portions of Chicken Balti for the freezer?

SERVES 4

INGREDIENTS	METRIC	IMPERIAL	AMERICAN
Chicken, skinned, boned and cubed	450 g	1 lb	1 lb
Onion, chopped	100 g	4 oz	1 cup
Garlic purée	5 ml	1 tsp	1 tsp
Ginger purée	5 ml	1 tsp	1 tsp
Tomato purée	5 ml	1 tsp	1 tsp
Balti Masala	15 ml	1 tbsp	1 tbsp
Ground cumin	5 ml	1 tsp	1 tsp
Turmeric	5 ml	1 tsp	1 tsp
Chilli powder	5 ml	1 tsp	1 tsp
Ground coriander	5 ml	1 tsp	1 tsp
Fenugreek leaves (optional)	5 ml	1 tsp	1 tsp
Whole green chillies	1-2	1-2	1-2
Balti sauce	450 ml	¾ pt	2 cups
Ghee or vegetable oil	50 g	2 oz	¼ cup
FOR THE GARNISH			
Fresh coriander leaves, chopped	15 ml	1 tbsp	1 tbsp
Balti Garam Masala	2.5 ml	½ tsp	½ tsp

1 Mix the dry spices with the tomato purée. Add a drop of vegetable oil if the paste is too dry. Set aside.

2 Heat the ghee in the karahi, and fry the onions until translucent. Add the ginger and garlic, and stir fry for 1 minute.

3 Add the spice paste and stir fry for 2 minutes.

4 Add the chicken pieces. Cook for 2-3 minutes, stirring continuously.

5 Pour in the Balti sauce, add the chillies, and bring to the boil. Then simmer for 25 minutes or until the sauce has reduced and thickened.

6 Remove from the heat, and sprinkle with Balti Garam Masala and fresh coriander.

SERVING SUGGESTION

Serve with naan bread, chick pea chutney and mango chutney.

Preparation time 5 minutes.

Cooking time 30 minutes.

CHICKEN, TOMATO AND FENUGREEK BALTI

Murgh Tomatar Methi Balti

A s you eat more Balti meals, you will start to understand how the different spices flavour your food, giving each dish a distinctive aroma and taste. This recipe is a traditionally cooked Balti and does not need a base sauce. It is suitable for freezing.

SERVES 4

INGREDIENTS	METRIC	IMPERIAL	AMERICAN
Chicken, skinned, boned and cubed	750 g	1½ lb	1½ lb
Onions, finely chopped	225 g	8 oz	8 oz
Garlic purée	5 ml	1 tsp	1 tsp
Ginger purée	5 ml	1 tsp	1 tsp
Fresh tomatoes, chopped	225 g	8 oz	8 oz
Green chillies	2	2	2
Fresh fenugreek leaves	30 ml	2 tbsp	2 tbsp
Fresh coriander leaves, chopped	30 ml	2 tbsp	2 tbsp
Balti Garam Masala	5 ml	1 tsp	1 tsp
Ghee	50 g	2 oz	¼ cup
Salt	to taste	to taste	to taste
SPICES			
Fennel seeds	2.5 ml	½ tsp	½ tsp
Mustard seeds	5 ml	1 tsp	1 tsp
Black cumin seeds	5 ml	1 tsp	1 tsp
Fenugreek seeds	2.5 ml	½ tsp	½ tsp
Onion seeds	2.5 ml	½ tsp	½ tsp
Whole black cardamoms	2	2	2
Whole green cardamoms, tops pinched	2	2	2
Chilli powder	5 ml	1 tsp	1 tsp
Ground coriander	5 ml	1 tsp	1 tsp
Ground cumin	5 ml	1 tsp	1 tsp

1. Dry fry the whole spices, then set them aside.

2. Heat the ghee and fry the onions until golden brown. Add the garlic and ginger, and fry for 1 minute.

3. Add the chopped tomatoes and stir fry until the tomatoes soften.

4. Stir in the whole and ground spices and salt. Cook for 2-3 minutes.

5. Mix in the fresh coriander and fenugreek leaves, then add the chicken and fresh chillies.

6. Cook for 25 minutes, stirring occasionally.

7. Remove from the heat. Sprinkle with Balti Garam Masala and serve.

SERVING SUGGESTION

Serve with aubergine (eggplant) chutney and a vegetable side dish.

Preparation time 8 minutes.

Cooking time 35 minutes.

BALTI CHICKEN PASANDA

Murgh Pasanda Balti

*T*his popular dish is served throughout Pakistan and Kashmir. The almonds in the sauce create a delicious nutty texture.

SERVES 4

INGREDIENTS	METRIC	IMPERIAL	AMERICAN
Chicken, boned and cubed	750 g	1½ lb	1½ lb
Onions, finely chopped	2	2	2
Fresh green chillies, chopped	2	2	2
Garlic purée	5 ml	1 tsp	1 tsp
Ginger purée	5 ml	1 tsp	1 tsp
Whole green cardamom	4	4	4
Balti Garam Masala	10 ml	2 tsp	2 tsp
Chilli powder	5 ml	1 tsp	1 tsp
Cassia bark	2.5 cm	1 in	1 in
Whole black peppercorns	6	6	6
Fresh coriander, chopped	30 ml	2 tbsp	2 tbsp
Ground almonds	15 ml	1 tbsp	1 tbsp
Natural yoghurt	120 ml	4 fl oz	½ cup
Single cream	120 ml	4 fl oz	½ cup
Ghee	50 g	2 oz	¼ cup

1 Melt the ghee and fry the onions until lightly browned.

2 Add the garlic and ginger, and fry for 1 minute. Then add the dry spices and fry for 2–3 minutes.

3 Mix in the chicken and stir fry for 5 minutes or until the chicken becomes dry.

④ Pour in the yoghurt and almonds, bring to the boil and simmer for 20 minutes.

⑤ Add the fresh coriander, chillies and cream. Cook for a further 5 minutes.

SERVING SUGGESTION

Serve with apple chutney, naan bread and a side dish of Potato, Okra and Aubergine Balti.

Preparation time 8 minutes.

Cooking time 35 minutes.

CHICKEN AND CUMIN BALTI

Balti Murgh Jeera

*P*opular for its aromatic qualities, cumin combines well with chicken in this mouth-watering Balti meal. It is suitable for freezing.

SERVES 4

INGREDIENTS	METRIC	IMPERIAL	AMERICAN
Chicken, skinned, boned and cubed	750 g	1½ lb	1½ lb
Onion, finely chopped	225 g	8 oz	8 oz
Fresh tomatoes, chopped	2	2	2
Balti sauce	450 ml	¾ pt	2 cups
Garlic purée	5 ml	1 tsp	1 tsp
Ginger purée	5 ml	1 tsp	1 tsp
Tomato purée	15 ml	1 tbsp	1 tbsp
Black cumin seeds	5 ml	1 tsp	1 tsp
White cumin seeds	5 ml	1 tsp	1 tsp
Ground cumin	15 ml	1 tbsp	1 tbsp
Balti Masala	10 ml	2 tsp	2 tsp
Cassia bark	5 cm	2 in	2 in
Whole green cardamoms	2	2	2
Fresh coriander leaves, chopped	45 ml	3 tbsp	3 tbsp
Ghee	50 g	2 oz	¼ cup

1 Melt the ghee in the karahi. Add the onions, ginger and garlic and fry for 2 minutes.

2 Add the spices and stir fry for 2–3 minutes without burning.

3 Stir in the fresh tomatoes and tomato purée, and fry until the tomatoes soften.

④ Add the chicken and cook for 5 minutes, stirring continuously.

⑤ Pour in the Balti sauce and bring to the boil. Turn the heat down and simmer for 20–30 minutes.

⑥ Stir in the fresh coriander leaves and cook for 1-2 minutes.

SERVING SUGGESTION

Serve with pan-fried puri or naan bread.

Preparation time 5 minutes.

Cooking time 35 minutes.

BALTI CHICKEN TIKKA MASALA

Murgh Tikka Masala

If you have some Chicken Tikka left over from your summer barbecue, this is a quick and easy way to create a sumptuous meal for your family and friends.

SERVES 4

INGREDIENTS	METRIC	IMPERIAL	AMERICAN
Chicken Tikka	450 g	1 lb	1 lb
Onion, finely chopped	100 g	4 oz	1 cup
Ginger purée	2.5 ml	½ tsp	½ tsp
Garlic purée	2.5 ml	½ tsp	½ tsp
Onion seeds	2.5 ml	½ tsp	½ tsp
Black cumin seeds	2.5 ml	½ tsp	½ tsp
Ghee	25 g	1 oz	2 tbsp
Masala sauce	450 ml	¾ pt	2 cups
Dried mint	2.5 ml	½ tsp	½ tsp
Single cream	15 ml	1 tbsp	1 tbsp

1. Melt the ghee and stir fry the onions until translucent. Add the spices and fry for 1 minute.

2. Add the garlic and ginger, and fry for 1 minute.

3. Add the Chicken Tikka and the Masala sauce, and simmer for 3–5 minutes.

4. Pour in the cream and sprinkle with mint. Simmer for 1–2 minutes.

SERVING SUGGESTION

Serve with plain boiled rice and crisp green salad.

Preparation time 5 minutes.

Cooking time 20 minutes.

BALTI CHICKEN WITH PEPPERS

*T*his is a rich, colourful Balti which is suitable for freezing.

SERVES 4

INGREDIENTS	METRIC	IMPERIAL	AMERICAN
Par-cooked chicken, cubed	750 g	1½ lb	1½ lb
Garlic purée	5 ml	1 tsp	1 tsp
Ginger purée	5 ml	1 tsp	1 tsp
Tomatoes, roughly chopped	450 g	1 lb	1 lb
Onions, sliced into rings	450 g	1 lb	1 lb
Red and green peppers, cut into strips	225 g	8 oz	8 oz
Green chillies, halved	2	2	2
Chilli powder	5 ml	1 tsp	1 tsp
Balti Masala	20 ml	4 tsp	4 tsp
Onion seeds	2.5 ml	½ tsp	½ tsp
Dried fenugreek leaves	5 ml	1 tsp	1 tsp
Salt	to taste	to taste	to taste
Ghee	50 g	2 oz	¼ cup

1 Melt the ghee in a karahi. Fry the ginger and garlic for 1-2 minutes, then add the chicken and stir fry for 5 minutes.

2 Add the dry spices and stir fry for 1–2 minutes.

3 Stir in the onions, tomatoes and salt. Cook for 5 minutes.

4 Add the peppers and fresh chilli, and cook for a further 5 minutes.

SERVING SUGGESTION

Serve with fresh chapatis and aubergine (eggplant) chutney.

Preparation time 5 minutes.
Cooking time 20 minutes.

BALTI BUTTER CHICKEN

Makhani Murgh Balti

*W*hen *you cook chicken in a spiced yoghurt sauce and then add cream towards the end of cooking, you create a delicious, creamy Balti dish. Unfortunately, it will be high in calories!*

SERVES 4

INGREDIENTS	METRIC	IMPERIAL	AMERICAN
Chicken breast, boned, skinned and diced	750 g	1½ lb	1½ lb
Onions, sliced thinly	2	2	2
Butter	75 g	3 oz	⅓ cup
Vegetable oil	15 ml	1 tbsp	1 tbsp
FOR THE SAUCE			
Yoghurt	150 ml	¼ pt	⅔ cup
Ginger purée	5 ml	1 tsp	1 tsp
Garlic purée	5 ml	1 tsp	1 tsp
Can tomatoes	225 g	8 oz	8 oz
Chilli powder	2.5 ml	½ tsp	½ tsp
Balti Garam Masala	30 ml	2 tbsp	2 tbsp
Whole green cardamoms	4	4	4
Salt	to taste	to taste	to taste
Ground almonds	50 g	2 oz	½ cup
Fresh coriander leaves, chopped	30 ml	2 tbsp	2 tbsp
Single cream	60ml	4 tbsp	4 tbsp

1 Blend together all the dry spices, yoghurt, ginger, salt, garlic and tomatoes.

2 Add the chicken, and set aside.

③ In the karahi, melt the butter and oil. Add the onions, and fry until translucent.

④ Add the chicken mixture. Bring to the boil, stirring continuously for 7–10 minutes.

⑤ Turn down the heat and simmer for 5 minutes. Then add half of the chopped coriander leaves and cook for 2–3 minutes.

⑥ Stir in the ground almonds and pour in the cream.

⑦ Garnish with the remaining chopped coriander leaves.

SERVING SUGGESTION

Serve with Lamb Biryani or plain pilau rice.

Preparation time 5 minutes.

Cooking time 25 minutes.

ORANGE AND CHICKEN BALTI

Orangi Murgh Balti

*T*he unusual combination of fresh orange and tomato in this Balti creates a refreshing flavour and an exciting colour. It is a real taste of sunshine!

SERVES 6

INGREDIENTS	METRIC	IMPERIAL	AMERICAN
Par-cooked chicken breast, cubed	900 g	2 lb	2 lb
Onion, sliced	225 g	8 oz	8 oz
Garlic purée	5 ml	1 tsp	1 tsp
Oranges, segmented	2	2	2
Can tomatoes, mashed with juice	400 g	14 oz	1¾ cups
Ground cumin	5 ml	1 tsp	1 tsp
Ground coriander	15 ml	1 tbsp	1 tbsp
Balti Masala	45 ml	3 tbsp	3 tbsp
Balti Garam Masala	15 ml	1 tbsp	1 tbsp
Fresh mint, chopped	15 ml	1 tbsp	1 tbsp
Fresh coriander, chopped	15 ml	1 tbsp	1 tbsp
Vegetable oil	15 ml	1 tbsp	1 tbsp
Butter	25 g	1 oz	2 tbsp

1 Heat the butter and oil in a karahi, and fry the chicken until golden brown.

2 Remove from the pan and drain.

3 Stir fry the onions and garlic for 3 minutes.

4 Add the spices and fry for 1-2 minutes, then stir in the remaining ingredients (leaving some mint and 2–3 orange segments for garnish) and bring to the boil.

5 Return the chicken to the pan and simmer for 20 minutes.

⑥ Garnish with a sprinkle of fresh mint and orange segments.

Preparation time 5 minutes.

Cooking time 30 minutes.

BALTI TURKEY WITH CORIANDER

Turkey Dhania Balti

Turkey is readily available throughout the year, not just at Christmas and Easter. This combination of turkey, fresh coriander and mint, will make a delightful change. The dish is suitable for freezing.

SERVES 4

INGREDIENTS	METRIC	IMPERIAL	AMERICAN
Turkey, skinned, boned and cubed	750 g	1½ lb	1½ lb
Onion, finely chopped	100 g	4 oz	1 cup
Fresh tomato, roughly chopped	1	1	1
Garlic purée	5 ml	1 tsp	1 tsp
Tomato purée	10 ml	2 tsp	2 tsp
Balti Masala	10 ml	2 tsp	2 tsp
Chilli powder	5 ml	1 tsp	1 tsp
Tandoori Masala	5 ml	1 tsp	1 tsp
Fresh coriander, chopped	30 ml	2 tbsp	2 tbsp
Fresh mint, chopped	30 ml	2 tbsp	2 tbsp
Balti sauce	300 ml	½ pt	1¼ cups
Lemon juice	10 ml	2 tsp	2 tsp
Ghee	50 g	2 oz	¼ cup
FOR THE GARNISH			
Balti Garam Masala	10 ml	2 tsp	2 tsp
Fresh coriander, chopped	15 ml	1 tbsp	1 tbsp

1 Mix together the dry spices and tomato purée to make a paste.

2 Heat the ghee, and fry the onions and garlic for 1 minute. Add the spice paste, then stir fry for 2–3 minutes.

③ Mix in the fresh coriander and mint, and add the turkey and tomato. Stir fry for 3–4 minutes.

④ Pour in the Balti sauce and lemon juice. Bring to the boil and then simmer for 25 minutes.

⑤ Remove from the heat. Sprinkle with Balti Garam Masala and fresh coriander leaves.

SERVING SUGGESTION

Serve with plain boiled rice and fresh coriander chutney.

Preparation time 5 minutes.

Cooking time 40 minutes.

BALTI LAMB ROGAN JOSH

Gosht Rogan Josh Balti

*I*nspired during the mogul reign, Rogan Josh has
been cooked for centuries in Kashmir as a celebra-
tion meal. To achieve the rich, dark red colour which is
the trade mark of this dish, many restaurants use a red
food colour. Instead we would suggest the (optional)
addition of fresh beetroot which is a natural colouring
agent. Do not use pickled beetroot. This dish is suitable
for freezing.

SERVES 4

INGREDIENTS	METRIC	IMPERIAL	AMERICAN
Par-cooked lamb, diced and trimmed	750 g	1½ lb	1½ lb
Onion, finely chopped	100 g	4 oz	1 cup
Red pepper, chopped	1	1	1
Fresh red chilli, chopped	1	1	1
Garlic purée	5 ml	1 tsp	1 tsp
Tomato purée	30 ml	2 tbsp	2 tbsp
Ghee or vegetable oil	50 ml	2 oz	3½ tbsp
Balti sauce	450 ml	¾ pt	2 cups
Ground almonds	25 g	1 oz	¼ cup
Fresh beetroot, peeled and grated	50 g	2 oz	½ cup
Fresh coriander leaves, chopped	15 ml	1 tbsp	1 tbsp
Salt	to taste	to taste	to taste
SPICES			
Tandoori Masala	5 ml	1 tsp	1 tsp
Paprika	5 ml	1 tsp	1 tsp
Ground bay leaves	1.5 ml	¼ tsp	¼ tsp
Whole cloves	4	4	4
Cassia bark	5 cm	2 in	2 in

INGREDIENTS	METRIC	IMPERIAL	AMERICAN
Whole green cardamoms, tops pinched	4	4	4
Whole black cardamoms	2	2	2
FOR THE GARNISH			
Fresh coriander leaves, chopped	15 ml	1 tbsp	1 tbsp
Flaked almonds	15 ml	1 tbsp	1 tbsp

1. Heat the ghee, and fry the onions and garlic until lightly browned.

2. Add the spices and fresh chilli, and stir fry for 2–3 minutes.

3. Stir in the lamb and cook for 5 minutes, stirring continuously.

4. Add the Balti sauce, beetroot, tomato purée, red pepper, coriander and almonds. Salt to taste.

5. Bring to the boil then simmer for 25 minutes or until the meat is tender.

6. Garnish with flaked almonds and fresh coriander.

Preparation time 5 minutes.

Cooking time 35 minutes.

NOTE:

Fresh chicken can replace par-cooked lamb in this dish.

KHARA LAMB BALTI

Khara Gosht Balti

This traditional karahi dish uses whole ('khara') spices, so remember to warn your dinner guests to pick out the whole spices before they start chewing!

SERVES 4

INGREDIENTS	METRIC	IMPERIAL	AMERICAN
Par-cooked lamb, cubed	450 g	1 lb	1 lb
Onions, sliced	2	2	2
Fresh tomatoes, chopped	2	2	2
Fresh green chillies, chopped	2	2	2
Fresh ginger, finely chopped	5 ml	1 tsp	1 tsp
Garlic cloves, sliced	2	2	2
Whole green cardamoms	4	4	4
Whole dried red chillies	4	4	4
Cassia bark	2 x 5 cm	2 x 2 in	2 x 2 in
Whole black peppercorns	6	6	6
Whole cloves	3	3	3
Salt	to taste	to taste	to taste
Vegetable oil	75 ml	5 tbsp	5 tbsp
Water	300 ml	½ pt	1¼ cups
Fresh coriander, chopped	30 ml	2 tbsp	2 tbsp

1 Heat the oil in a karahi. Add the onions and fry until lightly browned.

2 Stir in the garlic, salt, ginger and all the whole spices. Stir fry for 1–2 minutes.

3 Mix in the tomatoes and fresh chillies, and cook for 1–2 minutes. Add the lamb and stir fry for 5 minutes.

④ Pour in the water. Bring to the boil and simmer for 15 minutes.

⑤ Stir in the fresh coriander and continue stirring for 2-3 minutes.

⑥ The Balti is ready to serve when the oil has separated and risen to the surface.

Preparation time 7 minutes.

Cooking time 25 minutes.

NOTE:

If you are using fresh lamb rather than par-cooked lamb, simmer for 25 minutes instead of 15 minutes.

LAMB KORMA BALTI

Korma Gosht Balti

A mild and creamy dish, this Balti is ideal for those who prefer mildly spiced foods.

SERVES 4

INGREDIENTS	METRIC	IMPERIAL	AMERICAN
Par-cooked lamb, cubed	750 g	1½ lb	1½ lb
Balti sauce	450 ml	¾ pt	2 cups
Onion, finely chopped	225 g	8 oz	8 oz
Fresh green chillies, finely chopped	2	2	2
Balti Masala	15 ml	1 tbsp	1 tbsp
Ground coriander	5 ml	1 tsp	1 tsp
Ground cumin	5 ml	1 tsp	1 tsp
Fenugreek leaves	10 ml	2 tsp	2 tsp
Whole green cardamoms	4	4	4
Whole cloves	2	2	2
Cassia bark	5 cm	2 in	2 in
Salt	to taste	to taste	to taste
Double cream	150 ml	¼ pt	⅔ cup
Blanched almonds, chopped	50 g	2 oz	½ cup
Balti Garam Masala	5 ml	1 tsp	1 tsp
FOR THE GARNISH			
Flaked almonds	15 ml	1 tbsp	1 tbsp
Fenugreek leaves	15 ml	1 tbsp	1 tbsp

1 Melt the ghee and fry the onions until translucent. Stir in the spices, salt and fresh chillies, and fry for 1–2 minutes.

2 Add the par-cooked lamb and stir fry, making sure that the meat is well covered with the spice mix.

③ Pour in the Balti sauce. Bring to the boil then simmer, stirring continuously, for 10 minutes until the sauce has reduced and thickened.

④ Remove from the heat, and sprinkle with the Balti Garam Masala and almonds. Fold in the cream.

⑤ Return to the heat and stir for 1–2 minutes, without boiling.

⑥ Garnish with flaked almonds and fenugreek leaves.

SERVING SUGGESTION

Serve with plain boiled rice and naan bread.

Preparation time 6 minutes.

Cooking time 20 minutes.

LAMB DHANSAK

Dhansak Gosht Balti

*D*hansak is a style of cooking from the central-western states of India. This recipe has been cleverly adapted by the Balti chefs and is now regularly featured on restaurant menus. It is a delicious combination of spices, meat and pulses. For extra flavour and texture, try adding a few pineapple chunks. Dhansak is suitable for freezing.

SERVES 4

INGREDIENTS	METRIC	IMPERIAL	AMERICAN
Par-cooked lamb, cubed	750 g	1½ lb	1½ lb
Whole green chillies, chopped	3	3	3
Can of chick peas, drained	400 g	14 oz	1¾ cups
Balti sauce	300 ml	½ pt	1¼ cups
Balti Masala	30 ml	2 tbsp	2 tbsp
Chilli powder	5 ml	1 tsp	1 tsp
Whole green cardamoms, tops pinched	2	2	2
Black cumin seeds	5 ml	1 tsp	1 tsp
Lemon juice	25 ml	1½ tbsp	1½ tbsp
Pineapple juice	25 ml	1½ tbsp	1½ tbsp
Ghee	50 g	2 oz	¼ cup

1 Melt the ghee in a karahi, add the dry spices and most of the chillies, and stir fry for 1–2 minutes.

2 Add the lamb and fry with spices for 2–3 minutes. Pour in the Balti sauce, juices and chick peas.

③ Bring to the boil and simmer for 7–10 minutes, stirring every 1–2 minutes.

④ Sprinkle with the remaining fresh chillies and cook for 1–2 minutes.

Preparation time 5 minutes.

Cooking time 25 minutes.

NOTE:

If you prefer, you can use par-cooked chicken instead of par-cooked lamb in this dish.

BALTI LAMB AND SPINACH

Gosht Saag Balti

This traditional Punjabi dish has become a firm favourite with Balti addicts throughout Britain. If you do not have fresh spinach, you can use frozen spinach.

SERVES 4

INGREDIENTS	METRIC	IMPERIAL	AMERICAN
Par-cooked lamb, cubed	750 g	1½ lb	1½ lb
Fresh spinach, chopped	450 g	1 lb	1 lb
Onion, finely chopped	225 g	8 oz	8 oz
Fresh green chillies, chopped	2	2	2
Balti sauce	450 ml	¾ pt	2 cups
Garlic purée	5 ml	1 tsp	1 tsp
Ginger purée	5 ml	1 tsp	1 tsp
Balti Masala	30 ml	2 tbsp	2 tbsp
Chilli powder	5 ml	1 tsp	1 tsp
Salt	to taste	to taste	to taste
Ghee	50 g	2 oz	¼ cup

1. Melt the ghee in a karahi, and fry the onions until translucent.

2. Add the ginger and garlic, and stir fry for 1 minute.

3. Stir in the dry spices and continue frying for 1–2 minutes.

4. Add the lamb and stir fry for a further 5 minutes.

5. Pour in the Balti sauce, add salt and bring to the boil. Simmer for a further 7–10 minutes.

6 Stir in the spinach and fresh chillies, and cover. Cook for 2–3 minutes.

SERVING SUGGESTION

Serve with naan bread and plain boiled rice.

Preparation time 5 minutes.

Cooking time 15 minutes.

NOTE:

If you prefer, you can use par-cooked chicken instead of par-cooked lamb in this dish.

LAMB TIKKA MASALA BALTI

Gosht Tikka Masala Balti

*I*n this recipe, the subtle quality of spiced and tender Lamb Tikka is used to its full effect by combining with a creamy Masala sauce.

SERVES 4

INGREDIENTS	METRIC	IMPERIAL	AMERICAN
Lamb Tikka	450 g	1 lb	1 lb
Onion, finely chopped	100 g	4 oz	1 cup
Garlic purée	5 ml	1 tsp	1 tsp
Ginger purée	5 ml	1 tsp	1 tsp
Tomato purée	5 ml	1 tsp	1 tsp
Chilli powder	5 ml	1 tsp	1 tsp
Balti Masala	5 ml	1 tsp	1 tsp
Salt	to taste	to taste	to taste
Masala sauce	450 ml	¾ pt	2 cups
Single cream	15 ml	1 tbsp	1 tbsp
Fresh coriander leaves	30 ml	2 tbsp	2 tbsp
Ghee	50 g	2 oz	¼ cup

1 Heat the ghee and fry the onions until lightly browned. Add the ginger and garlic, and stir fry for 1 minute.

2 Add the dry spices, salt and tomato purée, and fry for 1–2 minutes.

3 Now add the Lamb Tikka and the Masala sauce, and simmer for 5–8 minutes.

4 Pour in the cream and sprinkle with fresh coriander.

Preparation time 5 minutes.

Cooking time 10 minutes.

BALTI LAMB BHUNA

Gosht Bhuna Balti

*B*huna is basically a method of dry cooking so you will only need to use a small amount of Balti sauce in this recipe. The dish is suitable for freezing.

SERVES 4

INGREDIENTS	METRIC	IMPERIAL	AMERICAN
Par-cooked lamb, cubed	750 g	1½ lb	1½ lb
Garlic purée	10 ml	2 tsp	2 tsp
Onion, chopped	225 g	8 oz	8 oz
Green pepper, roughly chopped	1	1	1
Chilli powder	5 ml	1 tsp	1 tsp
White cumin seeds	5 ml	1 tsp	1 tsp
Balti Masala	15 ml	1 tbsp	1 tbsp
Ground coriander	5 ml	1 tsp	1 tsp
Tomato purée	5 ml	1 tsp	1 tsp
Vegetable oil	5 ml	1 tsp	1 tsp
Balti sauce	250 ml	8 fl oz	1 cup
Balti Garam Masala	5 ml	1 tsp	1 tsp
Ghee	50 g	2 oz	¼ cup
FOR THE GARNISH			
Fresh coriander	15 ml	1 tbsp	1 tbsp

1. Make a paste using the dry spices (except the Balti Garam Masala), tomato purée and oil.

2. Heat the ghee in the karahi and fry the onions, pepper and garlic for 1–2 minutes. Stir in the spice paste and fry together for 2–3 minutes.

3. Add the meat and stir fry for 5 minutes, making sure that the meat is well covered by the Bhuna sauce.

4. Pour in the Balti sauce. Stir and simmer for 10 minutes. Stir in the Balti Garam Masala and serve.

Cooking time 20 minutes.

KASHMIRI LAMB MEATBALLS

Kashmiri Gosht Kofta

*T*hese small meatballs are flavoured with rich Balti spices and served with a creamy sauce. They are suitable for freezing.

SERVES 6

INGREDIENTS	METRIC	IMPERIAL	AMERICAN
FOR THE MEATBALLS			
Minced lamb	750 g	1½ lb	1½ lb
Garlic purée	7.5 ml	1½ tsp	1½ tsp
Ginger purée	20 ml	4 tsp	4 tsp
Red chilli, finely chopped	1	1	1
Balti Masala	30 ml	2 tbsp	2 tbsp
Chilli powder	5 ml	1 tsp	1 tsp
Fresh coriander, chopped	15 ml	1 tbsp	1 tbsp
Salt	to taste	to taste	to taste
Ghee	50 g	2 oz	¼ cup
FOR THE SAUCE			
Water or stock	50 ml	2 fl oz	3½ tbsp
Single cream	120 ml	4 fl oz	½ cup
Natural yoghurt	15 ml	1 tbsp	1 tbsp
Sugar	5 ml	1 tsp	1 tsp
Saffron strands	5 ml	1 tsp	1 tsp
Salt	to taste	to taste	to taste
Fresh coriander leaves, chopped	15 ml	1 tbsp	1 tbsp

1 In a bowl, mix together the minced lamb, ginger, garlic, fresh chilli, spices, salt and fresh coriander leaves.

② Shape into small balls around the size of a golf ball.

③ Meanwhile, soak the saffron in 1 tbsp of hot water.

④ Melt the ghee in the karahi and gently fry the meatballs until brown on all sides. Remove and drain on kitchen roll.

⑤ Using the karahi, stir in the cream, yoghurt, stock, sugar, saffron, salt and fresh coriander, until the mixture is simmering.

⑥ Add the cooked meatballs and simmer for 20 minutes. The sauce will thicken with cooking.

NOTE:

For Lamb Meatball Masala, use this recipe but replace the sauce mix with 450 ml/¾ pt of pre-cooked Masala sauce.

Preparation time 10 minutes.

Cooking time 35 minutes.

LAMB WITH APRICOT BALTI

Gosht Khubani Balti

*I*n this Persian-influenced dish, pieces of tender lamb are combined with dried fruit and almonds to create a delicious Balti meal for all the family.

SERVES 4

INGREDIENTS	METRIC	IMPERIAL	AMERICAN
Par-cooked lamb, trimmed and cubed	450 g	1 lb	1 lb
Onion, finely chopped	225 g	8 oz	8 oz
Garlic purée	7.5 ml	1½ tsp	1½ tsp
Ginger purée	15 ml	1 tbsp	1 tbsp
Balti Masala	30 ml	2 tbsp	2 tbsp
Ground aniseed	5 ml	1 tsp	1 tsp
Water or meat stock	175 ml	6 fl oz	¾ cup
Whole green cardamoms, tops pinched	3	3	3
Almonds, blanched	50 g	2 oz	½ cup
Can of prunes, stoneless and strained	75 g	3 oz	½ cup
Dried apricots	75g	3 oz	½ cup
Fresh coriander, chopped	15 ml	1 tbsp	1 tbsp
Ghee	50 g	2 oz	¼ cup

1 Melt the ghee, and fry the onions until golden brown. Add the ginger and garlic, and stir fry for 1–2 minutes.

2 Add the Balti Masala and ground aniseed, and stir fry until the mixture becomes aromatic.

3 Mix in the lamb pieces and stir fry for 5 minutes.

④ Pour in the water or stock and bring to the boil. Then turn down and simmer for 15 minutes, stirring frequently.

⑤ Add the almonds, prunes, apricots, cardamoms and fresh coriander. Continue cooking for 10 minutes.

SERVING SUGGESTION

Serve with plain pilau rice, naan bread or chapati.

Preparation time 5 minutes.

Cooking time 35 minutes.

MINCED BEEF, POTATO AND PEAS BALTI

Keema Aloo Balti

Keema Balti is a traditional dish served throughout Balti restaurants. It is a simple meal to prepare and cook.

SERVES 4

INGREDIENTS	METRIC	IMPERIAL	AMERICAN
Minced beef, lean	450 g	1 lb	1 lb
Onion, chopped	225 g	8 oz	8 oz
Potatoes, par-boiled and diced	450 g	1 lb	1 lb
Peas, frozen	50 g	2 oz	½ cup
Garlic purée	15 ml	1 tbsp	1 tbsp
Ginger purée	15 ml	1 tbsp	1 tbsp
Tomato purée	10 ml	2 tsp	2 tsp
Balti Masala	15 ml	1 tbsp	1 tbsp
Chilli powder	5 ml	1 tsp	1 tsp
Whole green chillies, chopped	2-3	2-3	2-3
Salt	to taste	to taste	to taste
Balti sauce	450 ml	¾ pt	2 cups
Ghee	50 g	2 oz	¼ cup
Balti Garam Masala	5 ml	1 tsp	1 tsp

1 Make a spice paste by mixing together the Balti Masala, chilli and tomato purée. Add a little oil if the paste is dry.

2 Melt the ghee in the karahi and stir fry the potatoes until brown. Remove and drain the potatoes and set aside.

③ In the karahi, fry the onions, garlic and ginger together. Add the spice paste and fresh chillies, and stir fry for 1–2 minutes.

④ Add the minced meat and salt. Fry until browned.

⑤ Pour in the Balti sauce, bring to the boil and simmer for 20 minutes, stirring occasionally.

⑥ Add the browned potatoes and frozen peas, and cook for 5 minutes.

⑦ Sprinkle with Balti Garam Masala and serve.

SERVING SUGGESTION

Serve with naan bread and sweet mango chutney.

Preparation time 10 minutes.

Cooking time 30 minutes.

LAMB BALTI

Balti Gosht

It is simple to cook this appetising and tasty dish. The aroma from the spices will certainly stimulate your taste buds!

SERVES 4

INGREDIENTS	METRIC	IMPERIAL	AMERICAN
Par-cooked lamb, cubed	750 g	1½ lb	1½ lb
Onion, chopped	225 g	8 oz	8 oz
Balti sauce	450 ml	¾ pt	2 cups
Ghee	50 g	2 oz	¼ cup
Balti Garam Masala	5 ml	1 tsp	1 tsp
FOR THE PASTE			
Garlic purée	5 ml	1 tsp	1 tsp
Tomato purée	5 ml	1 tsp	1 tsp
Balti Masala	10 ml	2 tsp	2 tsp
Ground cumin	5 ml	1 tsp	1 tsp
Ground coriander	5 ml	1 tsp	1 tsp
Turmeric	5 ml	1 tsp	1 tsp
Paprika	5 ml	1 tsp	1 tsp
Fresh coriander leaves, chopped	15 ml	1 tbsp	1 tbsp
Vegetable oil	5 ml	1 tsp	1 tsp
FOR THE GARNISH			
Fresh coriander leaves	15 ml	1 tbsp	1 tbsp
Tomato, cut into quarters	1	1	1

❶ Make a paste by mixing together all the spices, chopped coriander, garlic purée, tomato purée and vegetable oil.

2 Heat the ghee in the karahi, and fry the onions until translucent. Stir in the spice paste and fry for 1–2 minutes.

3 Add the lamb and stir fry for 5 minutes.

4 Pour in the Balti sauce. Bring to the boil and simmer for 20 minutes.

5 Sprinkle with Balti Garam Masala. Garnish with coriander leaves and fresh tomato.

SERVING SUGGESTION

Serve with naan bread, mint raita and apple chutney.

Preparation time 2–3 minutes.

Cooking time 30 minutes.

LAMB WITH FENUGREEK
. . . .
Methi Gosht Balti

*T*he combination of lamb and fresh fenugreek in this dish works extremely well. Fenugreek is an aromatic herb, which has been grown throughout Asia since ancient times. Its Latin name translates as 'Greek hay'. Fresh bunches of fenugreek ('methi') can be purchased in local Asian grocery shops. If you have difficulty buying fresh fenugreek, then use dried fenugreek instead (but halve the quantity in this recipe).

SERVES 4

INGREDIENTS	METRIC	IMPERIAL	AMERICAN
Par-cooked lamb, cubed	750 g	1½ lb	1½ lb
Onion, finely chopped	225 g	8 oz	8 oz
Garlic cloves, chopped	2	2	2
Fresh ginger, finely chopped	2.5 cm	1 in	1 in
Fresh tomatoes, chopped	2	2	2
Tomato purée	5 ml	1 tsp	1 tsp
Balti Masala	30 ml	2 tbsp	2 tbsp
Cassia bark	5 cm	2 in	2 in
Fresh fenugreek leaves, without stalks	15 ml	1 tbsp	1 tbsp
Fresh mint, chopped	15 ml	1 tbsp	1 tbsp
Balti sauce	450 ml	¾ pt	2 cups
Ghee	50 g	2 oz	¼ cup
Balti Garam Masala	5 ml	1 tsp	1 tsp
FOR THE GARNISH			
Fresh coriander	15 ml	1 tbsp	1 tbsp
Fenugreek leaves	15 ml	1 tbsp	1 tbsp

1. Heat the ghee and fry the onions, garlic and ginger for 2 minutes. Add the Balti Masala and cassia bark, and stir fry for 1 minute.

2. Stir in the chopped tomatoes and tomato purée, and fry gently until the tomatoes have softened.

3. Add the meat and cook for 5 minutes, stirring continuously.

4. Pour in the Balti sauce, fenugreek leaves and mint. Bring to the boil, and simmer for 15–20 minutes or until the sauce has thickened.

5. Remove from the heat and sprinkle with Balti Garam Masala.

6. Garnish with fresh coriander and fenugreek leaves.

Preparation time 7 minutes.

Cooking time 30 minutes.

BALTI BEEF MADRAS

Balti Gosht Madras

*M*adras *is a delicious hot curry from Southern India. It is not traditionally associated with recipes from the Northern regions, but, because of its popularity throughout Britain, the ingenious Balti chefs have come up with a Balti-style Madras. It is suitable for freezing.*

SERVES 4

INGREDIENTS	METRIC	IMPERIAL	AMERICAN
Par-cooked beef, cubed	750 g	1½ lb	1½ lb
Garlic cloves, chopped	3	3	3
Can tomatoes, drained	175 g	6 oz	¾ cup
Tomato purée	20 ml	4 tsp	4 tsp
Balti Masala	15 ml	1 tbsp	1 tbsp
Tandoori Masala	15 ml	1 tbsp	1 tbsp
Whole cloves	2	2	2
Whole green cardamoms, tops pinched	2	2	2
Chilli powder	5 ml	1 tsp	1 tsp
Ground cumin	5 ml	1 tsp	1 tsp
Whole red peppers, fresh or dried	2	2	2
Fresh green chillies, chopped	2	2	2
Sugar (optional)	5 ml	1 tsp	1 tsp
Salt	to taste	to taste	to taste
Balti sauce	450 ml	¾ pt	2 cups
Ghee	50 g	2 oz	¼ cup
FOR THE GARNISH			
Fresh coriander leaves	15 ml	1 tbsp	1 tbsp

1 Make a spice paste by combining the dry spices with the tomato purée.

2 Heat the ghee in the karahi, add the spice paste and fry for 1-2 minutes. Now add the garlic and stir fry for 1 minute.

3 Add the beef and continue to stir fry for about 5 minutes.

4 Pour in the Balti sauce.

5 Once the mixture is simmering, add the tomatoes, red peppers and green chillies, salt and sugar.

6 Simmer for a further 20 minutes.

SERVING SUGGESTION

Serve with plain boiled rice and a cooling cucumber raita.

Preparation time 5 minutes.

Cooking time 30 minutes.

BALTI LAMB DOPIAZA

Gosht Dopiaza Balti

A literal translation of 'dopiaza' is 'two onions'. *During the cooking process, onions are added to the dish in two separate ways: sliced onion is initially fried in the karahi, and then more onion is added within the Balti sauce. This dish is suitable for freezing.*

SERVES 4

INGREDIENTS	METRIC	IMPERIAL	AMERICAN
Par-cooked lamb, cubed	750 g	1½ lb	1½ lb
Onions, finely sliced	350 g	12 oz	12 oz
Garlic cloves, finely chopped	2	2	2
Balti Masala	5 ml	1 tsp	1 tsp
Chilli powder	5 ml	1 tsp	1 tsp
Cardamom seeds	1.5 ml	¼ tsp	¼ tsp
Black cumin seeds	5 ml	1 tsp	1 tsp
Paprika	5 ml	1 tsp	1 tsp
Balti sauce	450 ml	¾ pt	2 cups
Lemon juice	5 ml	1 tsp	1 tsp
Ghee	100 g	4 oz	½ cup

1 Heat the ghee in the karahi, and gently fry the onions until translucent. Add the garlic and fry for 1 minute.

2 Stir in the spices and fry for a further 1–2 minutes.

3 Add the lamb and stir fry for 3 minutes. Then pour in the Balti sauce and lemon juice, bring to simmering point, and cook for 10 minutes.

SERVING SUGGESTION

Delicious served with naan bread.

Preparation time 7 minutes.

Cooking time 15–20 minutes.

BALTI BEEF

I *t may seem extravagant to cook this Balti dish with rump or sirloin steak, but the extra cost really is worthwhile. Balti Beef can be frozen for future use.*

SERVES 4

INGREDIENTS	METRIC	IMPERIAL	AMERICAN
Rump steak, cubed	750 g	1½ lb	1½ lb
Onion, finely chopped	100 g	4 oz	1 cup
Garlic cloves, chopped	2	2	2
Balti Masala	15 ml	1 tbsp	1 tbsp
Fenugreek seeds	5 ml	1 tsp	1 tsp
Ground cumin	5 ml	1 tsp	1 tsp
Ghee	50 g	2 oz	¼ cup
Balti sauce	450 ml	¾ pt	2 cups
Fresh coriander, chopped	15 ml	1 tbsp	1 tbsp

1 Heat the ghee in a pan, and fry the onions and garlic together for 1-2 minutes.

2 Add the Balti Masala, fenugreek seeds and ground cumin and stir fry for a further 2-3 minutes.

3 Add the meat and stir fry for 8 minutes. Pour in the Balti sauce, bring to the boil and simmer for 35 minutes.

4 Garnish with fresh coriander.

SERVING SUGGESTION

Serve with a vegetable side dish and naan bread.

Preparation time 4 minutes.

Cooking time 40 minutes.

MINCED MEAT AND BLACK-EYED BEAN BALTI

Keema Lobia Balti

*F*or this dish, we have used tinned black-eyed beans as they require no pre-soaking or cooking. Combined with minced meat, they produce a substantial and tasty Balti for all the family.

SERVES 4

INGREDIENTS	METRIC	IMPERIAL	AMERICAN
Minced lamb or beef	450 g	1 lb	1 lb
Black-eyed beans, tinned and drained	400 g	14 oz	2 cups
Onion, chopped	225 g	8 oz	8 oz
Garlic purée	5 ml	1 tsp	1 tsp
Ginger purée	5 ml	1 tsp	1 tsp
Balti sauce	450 ml	¾ pt	2 cups
Black cumin seeds	5 ml	1 tsp	1 tsp
Cardamom seeds	2.5 ml	½ tsp	½ tsp
Fenugreek seeds	4 ml	¾ tsp	¾ tsp
Tandoori Masala	10 ml	2 tsp	2 tsp
Cassia bark	5 cm	2 in	2 in
Ghee	25 g	1 oz	2 tbsp
Balti Garam Masala	5 ml	1 tsp	1 tsp
Fresh coriander, chopped	15 ml	1 tbsp	1 tbsp

❶ Heat the ghee, and fry the onions until translucent. Add the garlic and ginger, then stir fry for a further 1 minute.

❷ Add all the spices except the Balti Garam Masala. Stir fry for 1-2 minutes.

③ Add the minced meat and cook for 5–7 minutes, stirring continuously.

④ Pour in the Balti sauce and beans, then bring to the boil. Turn down the heat and simmer for 20 minutes.

⑤ Sprinkle with Balti Garam Masala and stir in the fresh coriander leaves.

SERVING SUGGESTION

Serve with freshly-cooked chapatis or naan bread and sweet mango chutney.

Preparation time 10 minutes.

Cooking time 30 minutes.

BALTI MEAT AND POTATOES

Balti Gosht Aloo

This tasty dish can be served with a vegetable side dish and naan bread.

SERVES 4

INGREDIENTS	METRIC	IMPERIAL	AMERICAN
Par-cooked lamb or beef, cubed	750 g	1½ lb	1½ lb
Potatoes, par-boiled and cubed	450 g	1 lb	1 lb
Onion, chopped	225 g	8 oz	8 oz
Garlic purée	5 ml	1 tsp	1 tsp
Ginger purée	5 ml	1 tsp	1 tsp
Whole green cardamoms	4	4	4
Whole cloves	3	3	3
Balti Masala	30 ml	2 tbsp	2 tbsp
Turmeric	5 ml	1 tsp	1 tsp
Fresh coriander leaves	15 ml	1 tbsp	1 tbsp
Balti sauce	450 ml	¾ pt	2 cups
Ghee	100 g	4 oz	½ cup

1   Heat the ghee in the karahi, and fry the onions until golden brown. Add the ginger and garlic, and stir fry for 1–2 minutes.

2   Add the spices and coriander, then fry for 2 minutes.

3   Now add the meat and continue to stir fry for 5 minutes.

4   Pour in the Balti sauce and simmer for 15 minutes. Add the par-boiled potatoes and continue to cook until the sauce has reduced.

Preparation time 5 minutes.

Cooking time 35 minutes.

CHAPTER SIX

FISH & SHELLFISH

B alti restaurants tend to include a number of prawn dishes but very few fish Baltis on their menus.

In fact, fish and shellfish offer a variety of flavours and textures, and therefore make a tasty - and quick - alternative to meat and poultry Balti dishes.

PRAWN BALTI

Jhinga Balti

*T*his recipe uses frozen prawns because they need no preparation and are extremely quick to cook. If you do have a little extra time, try replacing the frozen prawns with fresh tiger prawns (peeled). Simply cook the dish for an extra 5 minutes.

SERVES 4

INGREDIENTS	METRIC	IMPERIAL	AMERICAN
Frozen prawns	600 g	1¼ lb	1¼ lb
Onion, finely chopped	100 g	4 oz	1 cup
Fresh tomato, chopped	1	1	1
Garlic purée	10 ml	2 tsp	2 tsp
Ginger purée	5 ml	1 tsp	1 tsp
Tomato purée	5 ml	1 tsp	1 tsp
Fresh green chillies, roughly chopped	2	2	2
Balti Masala	30 ml	2 tbsp	2 tbsp
Paprika	5 ml	1 tsp	1 tsp
Balti sauce	450 ml	¾ pt	2 cups
Ghee	50 g	2 oz	¼ cup
FOR THE GARNISH			
Fresh coriander leaves, chopped	15 ml	1 tbsp	1 tbsp
Balti Garam Masala	2.5 ml	½ tsp	½ tsp

1 Heat the ghee and fry the onions until translucent. Add the ginger and garlic, and stir fry for 30 seconds.

2 Add the dry spices and tomato purée, and stir fry for 1 minute.

③ Add the fresh tomato and chillies. Stir fry for 1-2 minutes until the tomato is soft.

④ Pour in the Balti sauce and bring to the boil. Lower the heat and simmer for 10 minutes.

⑤ Stir in the prawns and cook for a further 5 minutes.

⑥ Remove from the heat and sprinkle with Balti Garam Masala and fresh coriander. Leave to rest for 1-2 minutes before serving.

Preparation time 5 minutes.

Cooking time 15–20 minutes.

MOGUL KING PRAWN BALTI

Mogul Shaar Jhinga Balti

*T*his mogul influenced dish, with its rich sauce and
flavours of the East, brings to mind the very essence
of Balti.

SERVES 4

INGREDIENTS	METRIC	IMPERIAL	AMERICAN
Freshwater king prawns, uncooked and peeled	450 g	1 lb	1 lb
Onion, finely chopped	1	1	1
Fresh tomatoes, chopped	3-4	3-4	3-4
Garlic purée	5 ml	1 tsp	1 tsp
Ginger purée	5 ml	1 tsp	1 tsp
Whole green chillies	2	2	2
Green pepper, roughly chopped	1	1	1
Bay leaf	1	1	1
Curry leaves	4-6	4-6	4-6
Whole green cardamoms, tops pinched	6	6	6
Whole cloves	6	6	6
Paprika	5 ml	1 tsp	1 tsp
Ground cumin	5 ml	1 tsp	1 tsp
Chilli powder	12.5 ml	2½ tsp	2½ tsp
Fenugreek seeds	1.5 ml	¼ tsp	¼ tsp
Balti sauce	450 ml	¾ pt	2 cups
Ghee	50 g	2 oz	¼ cup
Fresh coriander, chopped	15 ml	1 tbsp	1 tbsp
Salt	to taste	to taste	to taste
Balti Garam Masala	5 ml	1 tsp	1 tsp

①   Heat the ghee in a karahi, add the onion and garlic, and gently fry until the onions are translucent.

②   Add the ginger purée, dry and whole spices – except the cardamoms – and gently fry for 1–2 minutes.

③   Add the tomatoes. Simmer until the tomatoes are reduced to a sauce.

④   Add the green pepper, salt and coriander leaves. Pour in the Balti sauce and simmer. Now add the cardamom pods and fresh chillies.

⑤   Simmer for around 30 minutes until the sauce has reduced, then add the prawns and continue cooking until the prawns are pink in colour. Sprinkle the Balti Garam Masala and cook for a further 5 minutes.

⑥   Leave the Balti to rest for 5 minutes before serving.

SERVING SUGGESTION

Serve in a traditional kadoi, garnished with a sprinkle of fresh coriander.

Preparation time 10 minutes.

Cooking time 35 minutes.

BALTI FISH MASALA

Machchi Masala Balti

This recipe combines Masala sauce with delicious Tandoori Fish (see recipe in Starters section), creating a smooth and tasty restaurant-style Balti.

SERVES 4

INGREDIENTS	METRIC	IMPERIAL	AMERICAN
Tandoori Fish	750 g	1½ lb	1½ lb
Onion, finely chopped	100 g	4 oz	1 cup
Fresh tomato, chopped	1	1	1
Garlic purée	5 ml	1 tsp	1 tsp
Ginger purée	5 ml	1 tsp	1 tsp
Tomato purée	5 ml	1 tsp	1 tsp
Balti Garam Masala	5 ml	1 tsp	1 tsp
Chilli powder	5 ml	1 tsp	1 tsp
Paprika	5 ml	1 tsp	1 tsp
Salt	to taste	to taste	to taste
Masala Sauce	450 ml	¾ pt	2 cups
Vegetable oil	30 ml	2 tbsp	2 tbsp
Cream	15 ml	1 tbsp	1 tbsp
Fenugreek leaves	15 ml	1 tbsp	1 tbsp

1 Mix together the dry spices, then blend them with tomato purée to make a smooth paste. Add a touch of oil if the paste is too dry.

2 Heat the oil and gently fry the onions, tomatoes, ginger and garlic for 2–3 minutes. Mix in the spice paste and stir fry for 2 minutes.

③ Pour in the Masala sauce and salt, and simmer for 10 minutes.

④ Add the Tandoori Fish. Cook for a further 5–7 minutes.

⑤ Sprinkle with fenugreek leaves and stir in the cream.

Preparation time 5 minutes.

Cooking time 15 minutes.

PRAWN, POTATO AND SPINACH BALTI

Jhinga Aloo Saag Balti

Full of texture, colour and flavours, this karahi-cooked dish is a must for those who love to entertain. You can use frozen instead of fresh spinach if you prefer.

SERVES 4

INGREDIENTS	METRIC	IMPERIAL	AMERICAN
Frozen prawns, defrosted	450 g	1 lb	1 lb
Fresh spinach, finely chopped	450 g	1 lb	1 lb
Onions, finely chopped	225 g	8 oz	8 oz
Par-boiled potatoes	450 g	1 lb	1 lb
Fresh tomatoes, chopped	450 g	1 lb	1 lb
Green chilli, finely chopped	1	1	1
Garlic purée	15 ml	1 tbsp	1 tbsp
Ginger purée	15 ml	1 tbsp	1 tbsp
Black mustard seeds	5 ml	1 tsp	1 tsp
Fenugreek seeds	5 ml	1 tsp	1 tsp
White cumin seeds	5 ml	1 tsp	1 tsp
Chilli powder	5 ml	1 tsp	1 tsp
Ground coriander	2.5 ml	½ tsp	½ tsp
Turmeric	2.5 ml	½ tsp	½ tsp
Mustard oil	75 ml	5 tbsp	5 tbsp
Vegetable oil	30 ml	2 tbsp	2 tbsp
Salt	to taste	to taste	to taste
FOR THE GARNISH			
Balti Garam Masala	5 ml	1 tsp	1 tsp
Fresh coriander, chopped	15 ml	1 tbsp	1 tbsp

1. Heat the oils in a karahi, then fry the onions until golden brown.

2. Stir in the mustard, cumin and fenugreek seeds, then add the garlic and ginger, and fry for 1 minute.

3. Add the ground spices and salt, and fry for 1 minute. Stir in the tomatoes until they soften.

4. Now add the potatoes and cook for 5-7 minutes. (If necessary, add 1-2 tbsp water to avoid sticking.)

5. Stir in the spinach, cover and cook for 5 minutes. Add the prawns and cook for a further 3-5 minutes.

6. Add the fresh chilli and cook for another minute, stirring continuously.

7. Sprinkle with Balti Garam Masala and fresh coriander before serving.

Preparation time 10 minutes.

Cooking time 20 minutes.

FISH & SHELLFISH

FISH BALTI

Machchi Balti

*W*hen preparing Fish Balti, it is better to cook the fish either whole or in steaks as smaller pieces tend to break up in the cooking process. For this recipe, you can use any variety of firm white fish, such as cod. This is a mild Balti so, if you prefer, you can add a couple of chopped fresh green chillies to make it more spicy.

SERVES 4

INGREDIENTS	METRIC	IMPERIAL	AMERICAN
Cod, cut into 10 cm/4 in pieces	750 g	1½ lb	1½ lb
Garlic purée	15 ml	1 tbsp	1 tbsp
Ginger purée	15 ml	1 tbsp	1 tbsp
Balti Masala	30 ml	2 tbsp	2 tbsp
Ground coriander	15 ml	1 tbsp	1 tbsp
Natural yoghurt	45 ml	3 tbsp	3 tbsp
Vegetable oil	30 ml	2 tbsp	2 tbsp
Salt	to taste	to taste	to taste
FOR THE GARNISH			
Fresh coriander, chopped	30 ml	2 tbsp	2 tbsp
Balti Garam Masala	5 ml	1 tsp	1 tsp

1 Heat the oil and add the ginger and garlic. Fry for 1–2 minutes.

2 Add the ground spices and salt, then stir fry for 4–5 minutes.

3 Pour in the yoghurt and stir well. Cook until the oil separates and rises to the surface.

112

④ Carefully add the fish pieces, and cook gently for 7–10 minutes.

⑤ Remove from the heat and sprinkle with Balti Garam Masala and fresh coriander.

SERVING SUGGESTION

Serve with sweet mango chutney and a chapati.

Preparation time 7 minutes.

Cooking time 20 minutes.

PRAWN DOPIAZA

Jhinga Dopiaza

A packet of prawns, Balti spices and a few onions
make this an economical and easy dish to serve.

SERVES 4

INGREDIENTS	METRIC	IMPERIAL	AMERICAN
Frozen prawns, defrosted	450 g	1 lb	1 lb
Onions, finely sliced	275 g	10 oz	10 oz
Garlic purée	10 ml	2 tsp	2 tsp
Tomato purée	10 ml	2 tsp	2 tsp
Salt	to taste	to taste	to taste
Balti Masala	10 ml	2 tsp	2 tsp
Black cumin seeds	5 ml	1 tsp	1 tsp
Chilli powder	5 ml	1 tsp	1 tsp
Ghee	50 g	2 oz	¼ cup
FOR THE GARNISH			
Fresh coriander	15 ml	1 tbsp	1 tbsp

1. Heat the ghee and fry 5 oz of onions until golden brown.

2. Add the garlic, tomato, salt and dry spices, and stir fry for 2–3 minutes.

3. Mix in the prawns and continue stir frying for 5 minutes.

4. Now add the remaining onions and cook on a low heat for a further 10 minutes.

SERVING SUGGESTION

Garnish with fresh coriander, and serve with coriander chutney.

Preparation time 7 minutes.

Cooking time 15–20 minutes.

BALTI LAKE FISH

Satpara Lake Fish

On a hot summer day, nothing beats fresh trout, lightly marinated with a blend of Balti spices.

SERVES 2

INGREDIENTS	METRIC	IMPERIAL	AMERICAN
Whole trout, medium sized, scales removed	2	2	2
FOR THE MARINADE			
Salt	5 ml	1 tsp	1 tsp
Chilli powder	5 ml	1 tsp	1 tsp
Balti Garam Masala	30 ml	2 tbsp	2 tbsp
Vegetable oil	30 ml	2 tbsp	2 tbsp
Lemon juice	60 ml	4 tbsp	4 tbsp

1 Blend the marinade ingredients together.

2 Make slits on both sides of the fish and rub in the mixture. Leave in a cool place for 30 minutes.

3 Grill the fish for 5–7 minutes on each side.

SERVING SUGGESTION

Serve with green salad and chutney.

Preparation time 5 minutes.

Marinating time 30 minutes.

Cooking time 10–15 minutes.

BALTI FRIED BATTERED FISH

This is a delicious Balti alternative to fish and chips.

SERVES 4

INGREDIENTS	METRIC	IMPERIAL	AMERICAN
Cod, filleted	750 g	1½ lb	1½ lb
Plain flour	50 ml	3½ tbsp	3½ tbsp
FOR THE BATTER			
Gram flour	100 g	4 oz	1 cup
Balti Garam Masala	15 ml	1 tbsp	1 tbsp
Balti Masala	30 ml	2 tbsp	2 tbsp
Lovage seeds	5 ml	1 tsp	1 tsp
Garlic purée	5 ml	1 tsp	1 tsp
Vinegar	15 ml	1 tbsp	1 tbsp
Natural yoghurt	45 ml	3 tbsp	3 tbsp
FOR FRYING			
Vegetable oil	375 ml	13 fl oz	1½ cups

1 Cut the cod into 10–12 cm/4–5 inch pieces

2 Sift the gram flour into a bowl, then mix in the other batter ingredients to make a thick, smooth batter.

3 Heat the oil in a deep pan or karahi. To check the oil is hot enough, drop in a small piece of bread. This should sizzle and rise to the surface.

4 Dip the fish pieces in the plain flour, then in the batter, making sure that each piece is well coated with batter mix.

⑤ Gently lower 2–3 pieces of fish into the oil and cook until golden brown.

⑥ Drain them on kitchen paper and serve whilst crisp.

SERVING SUGGESTION

Serve on a freshly cooked chapati, with mint raita.

Preparation time 10 minutes.

Cooking time 15 minutes.

PRAWNS, SPRING ONIONS AND CORIANDER

Jhinga Dhania Haya Piaz

The addition of spring onions and fresh coriander give this traditional dish a fresh and tangy flavour. You can use pre-cooked or frozen prawns (defrosted).

SERVES 4

INGREDIENTS	METRIC	IMPERIAL	AMERICAN
Prawns, peeled	450 g	1 lb	1 lb
Onions, finely chopped	175 g	6 oz	6 oz
Fresh tomatoes, chopped	225 g	8 oz	8 oz
Fresh red chilli, finely chopped	1	1	1
Spring onions, chopped	1 bunch	1 bunch	1 bunch
Ginger purée	10 ml	2 tsp	2 tsp
Garlic purée	5 ml	1 tsp	1 tsp
Balti Masala	10 ml	2 tsp	2 tsp
Chilli powder	5 ml	1 tsp	1 tsp
Fresh coriander, chopped	75 ml	5 tbsp	5 tbsp
Mustard oil	45 ml	3 tbsp	3 tbsp
Vegetable oil	15 ml	1 tbsp	1 tbsp
Salt	to taste	to taste	to taste

1. Heat the oils and fry the onions until golden brown. Add the garlic, ginger and dry spices, and fry for 2–3 minutes.

2. Pour in the tomatoes and stir fry until soft. If the mixture sticks, add 1 tbsp water. Add the prawns and salt, then cook on a medium heat for 5 minutes.

3. Stir in the spring onions, fresh chilli and fresh coriander, then serve.

Preparation time 8 minutes.

Cooking time 10-15 minutes.

CHAPTER SEVEN

VEGETABLES AND PULSES

An enormous variety of vegetables is grown throughout Baltistan and Kashmir. In the high mountainous areas of the region where the winters are long and cold, vegetables that have been dried during the summer months are cooked with spices to create an array of mouth-watering Balti dishes. Famous for its beautiful lakes and waterways, Kashmir has an abundance of cucumbers, tomatoes, mint and mushrooms – all of which can be used in Balti dishes.

Originating in India, lentils are rich in proteins and easily digested. They are recognised as one of the oldest known food sources, and today they form an essential element in a vegetarian diet. Lentils grow very quickly, propagating in three months. They can be dried and stored for use at a later date. In Balti cuisine, lentils are often combined with meat, vegetables and poultry to add texture and taste. Lentil dishes will complement a range of Balti main courses or they can form a complete meal in themselves.

If you are feeling imaginative, then this is your chance to experiment with a combination of your favourite vegetables and pulses, a few teaspoons of Balti Masala, a portion of Balti sauce, and lots of fresh coriander. You will be amazed by your own creativity!

You can also cook vegetarian versions of the meat Balti dishes included in this book. Try replacing the meat with Paneer. This is a vegetarian cheese-like substance which will add extra flavour to the dish. You can buy ready-made Paneer at an Asian supermarket.

All the vegetable dishes here can be served as main or side dishes. When cooking any of these recipes as a side dish, halve the quantities listed below.

ONION SEED CAULIFLOWER BALTI

Gobi Kilongi Balti

The flavours of cauliflower are delicately enhanced by the addition of onion seeds in this traditionally cooked Balti dish.

SERVES 4

INGREDIENTS	METRIC	IMPERIAL	AMERICAN
Cauliflower florets	450 g	1 lb	1 lb
Ghee or vegetable oil	30 ml	2 tbsp	2 tbsp
Onion seeds	2.5 ml	½ tsp	½ tsp
Turmeric	1.5 ml	¼ tsp	¼ tsp
Paprika	2.5 ml	½ tsp	½ tsp
Fresh green chillies, finely sliced	2	2	2
Salt	to taste	to taste	to taste

1 Heat the ghee or oil in the karahi.

2 Fry the onion seeds, turmeric and chillies for 2–3 minutes or until you can smell the aromatic fragrance.

3 Add the cauliflower florets, paprika and salt. Stir well so that the florets are well coated with the aromatic oil.

4 Lower the heat and cook for 10–12 minutes or until tender. If the cauliflower starts to stick, add 1 tbsp of water.

Preparation time 5 minutes.

Cooking time 10–15 minutes.

CHICK PEA BALTI

Kabli Chana Balti

*A*lthough chick peas are naturally quite bland in flavour, they make a tangy and delicious vegetarian Balti when cooked with ginger, tomatoes and Balti spices. This dish is suitable for freezing.

SERVES 4

INGREDIENTS	METRIC	IMPERIAL	AMERICAN
Chick peas, tinned and drained	400 g	14 oz	2½ cups
Onion, finely chopped	225 g	8 oz	8 oz
Fresh green chillies, roughly chopped	3	3	3
Medium tomatoes, chopped	3	3	3
Ginger purée	10 ml	2 tsp	2 tsp
Garlic purée	5 ml	1 tsp	1 tsp
Balti Masala	30 ml	2 tbsp	2 tbsp
Mango powder (optional)	5 ml	1 tsp	1 tsp
Ground black pepper	2.5 ml	½ tsp	½ tsp
Water	75 ml	5 tbsp	5 tbsp
Ghee	50 g	2 oz	¼ cup
Salt	to taste	to taste	to taste
Lemon juice	15 ml	1 tbsp	1 tbsp
Fresh coriander, chopped	15 ml	1 tbsp	1 tbsp
Mushrooms, sliced (optional)	225g	8 oz	8 oz

1 Heat the ghee and gently fry the onions, ginger and garlic until lightly browned.

2 Add the tomatoes, fresh chilli and dry spices. Cook for 5 minutes.

3 Add the chick peas, water and mushrooms (optional). Salt to taste.

4 Simmer for 5 minutes.

SERVING SUGGESTION

Sprinkle with lemon juice and fresh coriander. Serve with naan bread, kebabs or Fish Balti.

Preparation time 8 minutes.

Cooking time 15 minutes.

RED LENTIL BALTI

Masoor Dhal Balti

*R*ed lentils are one of the oldest known food-stuffs. Used throughout Asia for curries and soups, they do not need soaking and are quick to cook.

SERVES 4

INGREDIENTS	METRIC	IMPERIAL	AMERICAN
Red lentils, dried ('masoor dhal')	450 g	1 lb	2⅔ cups
Ginger purée	5 ml	1 tsp	1 tsp
Garlic purée	5 ml	1 tsp	1 tsp
Balti Masala	10 ml	2 tsp	2 tsp
Chilli powder	5 ml	1 tsp	1 tsp
Salt	5 ml	1 tsp	1 tsp
Water	1 l	1¾ pt	4¼ cups
FOR THE BAGHUR (GARNISH)			
Ghee	50g	2 oz	¼ cup
Onion, chopped	225 g	8 oz	8 oz
Lemon juice	15 ml	1 tbsp	1 tbsp
Fresh coriander, chopped	15 ml	1 tbsp	1 tbsp

1 Put the rinsed lentils in a pan with the ginger, garlic, salt and dry spices, and combine with enough water to cover them.

2 Bring to the boil and simmer for 30 minutes or until tender.

3 In a pan, heat the ghee and gently fry the onions until golden brown.

4 Pour the onion and oil mixture over the cooked lentils.

⑤ Sprinkle with lemon juice and garnish with fresh coriander leaves.

Preparation time 2–3 minutes.

Cooking time 30 minutes.

NOTE:

For extra flavour, fry the onions with 1 tsp cumin seeds, 2 whole red chillies and 2–3 curry leaves.

POTATO, OKRA AND AUBERGINE BALTI

Aloo Bindi Brinjal Balti

*T*his is quite a dry Balti. The combination of aubergines, okra and potatoes makes an interesting and tasty dish, with a distinctive flavour and texture.

SERVES 4

INGREDIENTS	METRIC	IMPERIAL	AMERICAN
Onions, finely chopped	225 g	8 oz	8 oz
Garlic purée	5 ml	1 tsp	1 tsp
Ginger purée	5 ml	1 tsp	1 tsp
Tomato purée	5 ml	1 tsp	1 tsp
Okra, topped	175 g	6 oz	6 oz
Baby aubergines (eggplants), cubed	175 g	6 oz	6 oz
Potatoes, cubed and par-boiled	275 g	10 oz	10 oz
Balti Garam Masala	10 ml	2 tsp	2 tsp
Black mustard seeds	5 ml	1 tsp	1 tsp
Asafoetida powder	pinch	pinch	pinch
Paprika	5 ml	1 tsp	1 tsp
Fresh coriander, chopped	15 ml	1 tbsp	1 tbsp
Fresh green chilli, chopped	1	1	1
Vegetable oil	5 ml	1 tsp	1 tsp
Water	150 ml	¼ pt	⅔ cup
Ghee	25 g	1 oz	2 tbsp
FOR THE GARNISH			
Fresh coriander, use a sprig	1	1	1
Tomato, sliced	1	1	1

❶ In a small bowl, mix together the dry spices, tomato purée and vegetable oil to make a paste.

2. Melt the ghee in a karahi and fry the onions until translucent.

3. Add the ginger and garlic purée and stir fry for 1 minute.

4. Stir in the spice paste, fresh chilli and coriander. Fry for 1-2 minutes. Add a splash of water if sticking occurs.

5. Add par-boiled potatoes, okra and aubergines. Stir fry into the paste mix, making sure all the vegetables have been coated. Cook for 2-3 minutes.

6. Pour in the water and bring to the boil. Turn down the heat and simmer for 20 minutes.

SERVING SUGGESTION

Garnish with fresh coriander and sliced tomato. Ideal side dish for Chicken or Lamb Balti.

Preparation time 8 minutes.

Cooking time 25 minutes.

POTATO BALTI

....

Balti Aloo

P otato easily absorbs the flavours of spices and so it is an ideal vegetable to use for a Balti side dish. Served as a main dish, Balti Aloo is delicious with mango chutney and aubergine (eggplant) raita.

SERVES 4

INGREDIENTS	METRIC	IMPERIAL	AMERICAN
Potato, thickly sliced and par-boiled	450 g	1 lb	1 lb
Fresh tomatoes, chopped	225 g	8 oz	8 oz
Cumin seeds	5 ml	1 tsp	1 tsp
Ground coriander	5 ml	1 tsp	1 tsp
Chilli powder	5 ml	1 tsp	1 tsp
Balti Masala	5 ml	1 tsp	1 tsp
Salt	to taste	to taste	to taste
Fresh coriander leaves, chopped	15 ml	1 tbsp	1 tbsp
Ghee or vegetable oil	60 ml	4 tbsp	4 tbsp
Fresh green chillies, chopped (optional)	2	2	2
FOR THE GARNISH			
Balti Garam Masala	5 ml	1 tsp	1 tsp

1   Heat the ghee and fry the cumin seeds for 30 seconds.

2   Stir in the salt and dry spices, and fry for a further 30 seconds.

3   Add the potatoes and tomatoes. Bring to the boil and simmer until the potatoes are tender.

4   Stir in the fresh coriander and chillies.

SERVING SUGGESTION

Garnish with a sprinkle of Balti Garam Masala.

Preparation time 5 minutes.

Cooking time 10–15 minutes.

AUBERGINE BALTI

Brinjal Balti

*W*ith its regal colour and delightful texture, the aubergine is a popular choice in Balti cookery. This variation of Aubergine Balti is delicious to serve with a Keema Balti.

SERVES 4

INGREDIENTS	METRIC	IMPERIAL	AMERICAN
Aubergines (eggplants), cubed	450 g	1 lb	1 lb
Onion, finely chopped	225 g	8 oz	8 oz
Whole green chillies, chopped	2	2	2
Garlic purée	5 ml	1 tsp	1 tsp
Tomato purée	5 ml	1 tsp	1 tsp
Ground fennel	5 ml	1 tsp	1 tsp
Cumin seeds	5 ml	1 tsp	1 tsp
Balti Masala	10 ml	2 tsp	2 tsp
Balti sauce	300 ml	½ pt	1¼ cups
Ghee	25 g	1 oz	2 tbsp
Fresh coriander	15 ml	1 tbsp	1 tbsp

1 Melt the ghee in a pan. Add the onion and fry until translucent.

2 Stir in the garlic and tomato purée with the dry spices. Fry for 1–2 minutes.

3 Add the fresh chillies and aubergines, and stir fry for 2–3 minutes.

4 Pour in the Balti sauce and bring to the boil. Lower the heat and simmer for 10–15 minutes.

5 Stir in the fresh coriander and serve.

Preparation time 5–10 minutes.

Cooking time 25 minutes.

MUSHROOM BALTI

This is a delicious dry Balti. For best results, serve immediately after cooking.

SERVES 4

INGREDIENTS	METRIC	IMPERIAL	AMERICAN
Button mushrooms	450 g	1 lb	1 lb
Onions, finely chopped	100 g	4 oz	1 cup
Garlic clove, finely chopped	1	1	1
Ghee or vegetable oil	50 g	2 oz	¼ cup
Balti Masala	15 ml	1 tbsp	1 tbsp
Fresh coriander leaves	15 ml	1 tbsp	1 tbsp
Salt	to taste	to taste	to taste

1. Melt the ghee in a karahi.

2. Fry the onions and garlic until translucent.

3. Add the Balti Masala and fry for 1–2 minutes.

4. Add the mushrooms and salt to taste, stirring continuously.

5. Cook for 5 minutes then serve.

SERVING SUGGESTION

Garnish with fresh coriander leaves.

Preparation time 5 minutes.

Cooking time 7 minutes.

MIXED VEGETABLE BALTI

Sabzi Balti

*U*sing *a mixture of vegetables, you can create a sumptuous main course Balti meal for the whole family. For this recipe, try using potatoes, broccoli, green beans, peas, cauliflower florets, for example. To make your Balti look more appealing, choose different coloured vegetables. If you are running short of time, par-cook the vegetables together for 5 minutes.*

SERVES 4

INGREDIENTS	METRIC	IMPERIAL	AMERICAN
Mixed vegetables, cubed	750 g	1½ lb	1½ lb
Onion, finely chopped	225 g	8 oz	8 oz
Tomatoes, chopped	2	2	2
Garlic purée	5 ml	1 tsp	1 tsp
Ginger purée	5 ml	1 tsp	1 tsp
Tomato purée	5 ml	1 tsp	1 tsp
Balti Masala	20 ml	4 tsp	4 tsp
Ground coriander	5 ml	1 tsp	1 tsp
Paprika	5 ml	1 tsp	1 tsp
Salt	to taste	to taste	to taste
Balti sauce	450 ml	¾ pt	2 cups
Whole green chillies (optional)	2-3	2-3	2-3
Ghee	50 g	2 oz	¼ cup
FOR THE GARNISH			
Fresh coriander leaves	15 ml	1 tbsp	1 tbsp
Balti Garam Masala	2.5 ml	½ tsp	½ tsp

❶ Mix together the dry spices and purées to make a smooth paste. If it is a little dry, add 1 tsp of vegetable oil.

2 Heat the ghee. Fry the onions and spice paste together for 2-3 minutes.

3 Add the tomatoes and fold in the vegetables. Salt to taste. Stir fry for a further 5 minutes.

4 Pour in the Balti sauce and add the whole chillies.

5 Bring to the boil, lower the heat and simmer for 20 minutes or until the vegetables are firm yet tender.

6 Remove from the heat, and sprinkle with fresh coriander and Balti Garam Masala.

Preparation time 10 minutes.

Cooking time 25 minutes.

OKRA DOPIAZA

Bindi Dopiaza

Known as 'lady's fingers', okra is a very popular vegetable throughout the Asian continent. You should not wash okra, as the sap will make the vegetable slimy. This recipe is a traditional version, perfect for cooking at home.

SERVES 4

INGREDIENTS	METRIC	IMPERIAL	AMERICAN
Okra, topped	450 g	1 lb	1 lb
Fresh tomatoes, chopped	50 g	2 oz	½ cup
Onions, finely sliced	275 g	10 oz	10 oz
Garlic cloves, chopped	4	4	4
Balti Masala	5 ml	1 tsp	1 tsp
Cumin seeds	5 ml	1 tsp	1 tsp
Chilli powder	5 ml	1 tsp	1 tsp
Ghee	50 g	2 oz	¼ cup

1. Cut the okra into 2.5 cm/1 inch pieces.

2. Heat the ghee, and fry 150 g/5 oz of the onions until golden brown.

3. Add the tomatoes, garlic and dry spices, and stir fry for 2–3 minutes.

4. Now stir in the chopped okra and fry for 7–8 minutes.

5. Add the remaining onions and stir fry for a further 10 minutes.

Preparation time 5 minutes.

Cooking time 25 minutes.

CHAPTER EIGHT

BREADS

Flat unleavened breads are cooked traditionally throughout the Asian continent. They are eaten either as a side dish or as a snack with raita or chutney.

When cooking naan breads, you will need to allow extra time, say 1½ hours, for the raising agents to start working. However, there are numerous ready-made naans available from supermarkets, and these are definitely the easiest option for those impromptu Balti meals.

When cooking ready-made naans, brush with melted ghee or sprinkle a little water on the naan bread before heating. This will keep the naan moist during the heating period.

Of course, there is nothing like home-made breads; freshly-cooked chapati or puri breads really do add a delicious touch to your Balti meal. They are simple to prepare and cook, with hardly any time needed for raising.

NAAN BREAD

Naans are traditionally cooked in a clay tandoor oven. The bread achieves its 'tear drop' shape when it is thrown on to the side of the tandoor.

MAKES 8

INGREDIENTS	METRIC	IMPERIAL	AMERICAN
Plain white flour	450 g	1 lb	4 cups
Baking powder	5 ml	1 tsp	1 tsp
Salt	2.5 ml	½ tsp	½ tsp
Sugar	10 ml	2 tsp	2 tsp
Eggs	2	2	2
Milk	60 ml	4 tbsp	4 tbsp
Natural yoghurt	60 ml	4 tbsp	4 tbsp
Water	60 ml	4 tbsp	4 tbsp
Melted ghee	50 g	2 oz	¼ cup
Vegetable oil	7.5 ml	1½ tsp	1½ tsp
Balti Garam Masala	5 ml	1 tsp	1 tsp
Fenugreek leaves, crushed (optional)	15 ml	1 tbsp	1 tbsp
Fresh coriander leaves, chopped (optional)	15 ml	1 tbsp	1 tbsp

1 Beat the eggs, then add the sugar, salt, spices, baking powder, yoghurt and melted ghee. Mix well.

2 Sieve the flour into the mixture and stir well.

3 Gradually add the water and milk to form a soft dough. Knead for 1–2 minutes.

4 Coat the dough with the vegetable oil, and leave to rest for 20 minutes.

⑤ Divide the dough into eight parts. Sprinkle them with flour and roll them into small balls.

⑥ Roll out each ball into an 18 cm/7 inch disc.

⑦ Place on a baking tray in a pre-heated oven at 220°C/ 425°F/gas mark 7 for 3 minutes.

⑧ Wrap the naan in a tea-towel and store it in a warm place until the remaining naans are cooked.

Preparation time 20 minutes.

Standing time 20 minutes.

Cooking time 3–4 minutes.

CHAPATI

A chapati is a thin, flat unleavened bread, served either as a snack with raita and chutney or as a side dish with your main course. It is simple to prepare and is easily cooked on a tawa or flat, heavy-based frying pan.

SERVES 4

INGREDIENTS	METRIC	IMPERIAL	AMERICAN
Light wholemeal flour	450 g	1 lb	4 cups
Salt	1.5 ml	¼ tsp	¼ tsp
Water	250 ml	8 fl oz	1 cup
Flour for dusting	15 ml	1 tbsp	1 tbsp

1 Sieve the flour and salt.

2 Make a well in the centre, and gradually add water until a soft dough forms – not too wet and not too dry.

3 Knead the dough for 1-2 minutes. Cover with a damp cloth and set aside for 5 minutes.

4 Heat the tawa or frying pan.

5 Divide the dough equally into small balls and flatten with your hand.

6 Roll the balls into flat circles of about 20 cm/8 inches diameter.

7 Place each chapati on the tawa and cook for 1 minute. Whilst the chapati is cooking, pat the outer edge with a dry cloth.

8 Turn the chapati over and cook for a further minute. The chapati will rise like an inverted dish when turned.

Preparation time 5 minutes.

Standing time 5 minutes.

Cooking time 2-3 minutes.

PURI

Pan-fried Bread

*A*lso known as a 'roti', the puri is pan fried for flavour and texture. Puris are often served with vegetable and lentil Balti dishes.

SERVES 6

INGREDIENTS	METRIC	IMPERIAL	AMERICAN
Plain white flour	450 g	1 lb	4 cups
Water	175 ml	6 fl oz	¾ cup
Ghee	30 ml	2 tbsp	2 tbsp
Salt	to taste	to taste	to taste

1. Mix together the flour, water and salt. Knead the dough for 4–5 minutes and leave to rest for 5 minutes.

2. Split the dough into 6 equal balls and roll into disc shapes.

3. Melt the ghee on a tawa or frying pan. Add one puri at a time and fry over a medium heat.

4. Cook for 2 minutes or until the puri starts to fleck brown. Turn over and cook for a further 2 minutes.

5. Place the cooked puri in a warm place, and repeat the process for the others.

Preparation time 5 minutes.

Standing time 5 minutes.

Cooking time 12 minutes.

SERVING SUGGESTION

Prawn Puri is a very popular starter at Balti Restaurants. See earlier section on Starters.

KEEMA NAAN

. . . .

A naan stuffed with spicy minced lamb ('Keema') is delicious served with kebabs or raita and chutney. It is a tasty meal in itself.

MAKES 6

INGREDIENTS	METRIC	IMPERIAL	AMERICAN
FOR THE NAAN DOUGH			
See earlier recipe			
FOR THE STUFFING			
Minced lamb, lean	450 g	1 lb	1 lb
Ground coriander	15 ml	1 tbsp	1 tbsp
Garlic cloves, finely chopped	3	3	3
Fresh ginger, finely chopped	2.5 cm	1 in	1 in
Onion, finely chopped	75 g	3 oz	¾ cup
Ground cumin	10 ml	2 tsp	2 tsp
Balti Masala	5 ml	1 tsp	1 tsp
Mint leaves, crushed	5 ml	1 tsp	1 tsp
Fresh coriander leaves, chopped	15 g	½ oz	2 tbsp
Tandoori Masala	2.5 ml	½ tsp	½ tsp
Salt	to taste	to taste	to taste

1 Mix together all the ingredients for the filling.

2 Pre-heat the oven to 220°C/425°F/gas mark 7.

3 Put some greaseproof paper on to a baking sheet and rub some grease over it.

4 Make the naan dough, as described in the earlier recipe, and split into 6 portions.

(5) Flatten each portion of naan dough by stretching and patting.

(6) Place a portion of the filling in the centre of the flattened naan dough. Turn in the edges to seal, then flatten into a round shape.

(7) Dust with a little flour and roll out to a 13 cm/5 inch diameter disc.

(8) Place the naan breads on the baking sheet and brush with yoghurt.

(9) Bake for 9–10 minutes in the upper part of the oven.

Preparation time 20 minutes.

Cooking time 10 minutes.

STUFFED CHAPATI

. . . .

Bhare Chapati

*T*hese delicately filled chapatis are served as a snack or an appetising starter.

SERVES 4

INGREDIENTS	METRIC	IMPERIAL	AMERICAN
Light wholemeal flour	450 g	1 lb	4 cups
Water	175 ml	6 fl oz	¾ cup
Salt	to taste	to taste	to taste
FOR THE STUFFING			
Mashed potato	75 g	3 oz	⅓ cup
White cumin seeds	5 ml	1 tsp	1 tsp
Fresh coriander leaves, chopped	15 ml	1 tbsp	1 tbsp
Mango powder	2.5 ml	½ tsp	½ tsp

❶ Mix together the flour, water and salt. Knead to a firm dough and set aside for 5 minutes.

❷ In a bowl, mix together all the stuffing ingredients.

❸ Divide the dough into eight balls of equal size. On a floured surface, roll the dough pieces into discs of around 13 cm/5 inches diameter.

❹ Take one disc and spread a quarter of the filling over the top. Place a second disc over this and press the edges firmly together.

❺ Heat the tawa or flat frying pan over a medium heat.

❻ Without using oil, cook the chapati on both sides until golden brown.

Preparation time 10 minutes.

Standing time 15 minutes.

CHAPTER NINE

RICE

Traditionally Balti is eaten with bread alone. However, for a change, you may like to serve your Balti with rice as well. Remember there are no rules in Balti cooking - it is up to you!

Always remember to wash the rice thoroughly before cooking. You can cook rice by boiling or by the absorption method, depending on the rice you use. Follow the recipe instructions for the best results. If the rice is covered during cooking, only remove the lid when necessary. After cooking, gently separate the grains of rice with a fork.

PILAU RICE

Sada Pulao

F ried with onions and spices, this variety of pilau rice is delicious served with Balti Butter Chicken.

SERVES 4

INGREDIENTS	METRIC	IMPERIAL	AMERICAN
Basmati rice	350 g	12 oz	1½ cups
Onion, roughly chopped	100 g	4 oz	1 cup
Bay leaf	1	1	1
Whole cloves	4	4	4
Cassia bark	3-5 cm	1-2 in	1-2 in
Green cardamoms, tops pinched	4	4	4
Black cumin seeds	5 ml	1 tsp	1 tsp
Salt	to taste	to taste	to taste
Ghee	50 g	2 oz	¼ cup
Water	600 ml	1 pt	2½ cups

1 Rinse the rice thoroughly under running water.

2 Melt the ghee in a frying pan, and fry the onions until lightly browned.

3 Add the rice and spices, and stir fry until the rice turns a dark creamy colour.

4 Add the water and salt, and bring to the boil. Cover with the lid and reduce heat to simmering point.

5 Cook for 5-7 minutes.

6 Remove from the heat and wrap pan well with a tea-towel. Leave for 10-15 minutes.

Preparation time 5 minutes.

Cooking time 12 minutes.

Standing time 10–15 minutes.

NOTE:

For extra flavour and effect, soak 8–10 strands of saffron in 45 ml/3 tbsp warm water or milk, and pour over the cooked rice. Leave for 20 minutes. The rice will turn a delicate, soft yellow colour. If you do not have saffron strands, try adding 2.5 ml/½ tsp turmeric before cooking.

LAMB BIRYANI

. . . .

Balti Gosht Biryani

*U*sing pilau rice, this dish is cooked and prepared in
minutes. Chicken and Prawn Biryani dishes can be
cooked using the same method.

SERVES 4-6

INGREDIENTS	METRIC	IMPERIAL	AMERICAN
Par-cooked lamb, cubed	450 g	1 lb	1 lb
Plain pilau rice, cooked	350 g	12 oz	3 cups
Peas, frozen	50 g	2 oz	½ cup
Green chillies, finely chopped	2	2	2
Almonds, roughly chopped	6	6	6
Salt	to taste	to taste	to taste
Ghee	50 g	2 oz	¼ cup
Balti sauce	450 ml	¾ pt	2 cups

1 Heat the ghee in a karahi.

2 Add the lamb, peas, almonds, chillies and salt, and stir
fry for 2 minutes.

3 Add the pilau rice. Using a wooden spoon, gently roll
the rice and lamb mixture together.

4 In a separate pan, heat the Balti sauce to simmering
point.

5 Serve the rice and lamb, and pour over the Balti sauce.

SERVING SUGGESTION

Balti Biryani is an ideal side dish for Balti Chicken Korma.

Preparation time 5 minutes.

Cooking time 10 minutes.

BOILED RICE

*G*rown in Pakistan and Kashmir, and prized throughout the world for its supreme flavour, Basmati rice is the ideal rice to serve with Balti dishes.

In this recipe, we have used the absorption method because this best suits the long, delicate grains of Basmati rice.

SERVES 4

INGREDIENTS	METRIC	IMPERIAL	AMERICAN
Basmati rice	350 g	12 oz	1½ cups
Water	600 ml	1 pt	2½ cups
Salt	to taste	to taste	to taste

1   Rinse the rice thoroughly under running water.

2   Place the rice and water in a pan and add salt to taste.

3   Bring to the boil, then cover with a lid and simmer for 5–7 minutes.

4   Remove from the heat, and wrap the pan well with a tea-towel. Leave for 15 minutes.

5   When ready to serve, gently fork the rice to separate the grains.

Preparation time 3 minutes.

Cooking time 7 minutes.

Standing time 15 minutes.

Chutneys, Raitas & Salads

When served with your Balti meal, chutneys will add considerable zest. Using fresh vegetables or fruit and a little seasoning, chutneys are extremely simple to prepare. Once you have tried some of the recipes in this section, you will soon be inspired to create a tasty dip of your own.

Raitas are cooling yoghurt dips, served with starters and main dishes. Why not experiment by adding fresh grapes, chopped nuts and any combination of fresh, chopped vegetables?

We have also included in this section a simple salad recipe as an ideal side dish for your Balti.

TAMARIND AND ONION CHUTNEY

This crunchy sweet and sour chutney is delicious served with plain popadoms or samosas as a starter. You will need to soak the tamarind for 1½ hours before making the chutney, but the actual method of preparation is very quick and easy.

SERVES 4

INGREDIENTS	METRIC	IMPERIAL	AMERICAN
Tamarind, with seeds	100 g	4 oz	1 cup
Hot water	300 ml	½ pt	1¼ cups
Onion, finely chopped	1	1	1
Ground black pepper	2.5 ml	½ tsp	½ tsp
Chilli powder	2.5 ml	½ tsp	½ tsp
Sugar	5 ml	1 tsp	1 tsp
Mint sauce	5 ml	1 tsp	1 tsp
Salt	to taste	to taste	to taste

1 Soak the tamarind in the hot water for 1½ hours.

2 Pour the soaked tamarind and its liquid through a sieve, pushing as much of the juice through the sieve as possible.

3 Discard the remaining pulp.

4 Now add the remaining ingredients to the tamarind juice.

5 Refrigerate for 30 minutes and serve.

Preparation time 5 minutes.

Standing time 1½ hours.

Chill time 30 minutes.

AUBERGINE CHUTNEY

Brinjal Chatni

If you want to give this tasty chutney some extra flavour, try cooking the aubergines on a charcoal barbecue.

SERVES 4

INGREDIENTS	METRIC	IMPERIAL	AMERICAN
Aubergines (eggplants)	750 g	1½ lb	1½ lb
Fresh green chillies	2-3	2-3	2-3
Coconut cream	50 g	2 oz	¼ cup
Fresh ginger	2.5 cm	1 in	1 in
Salt	to taste	to taste	to taste
Lime juice	7.5 ml	1½ tsp	1½ tsp
Fresh coriander leaves, chopped	15 ml	1 tbsp	1 tbsp
Vegetable oil	15 ml	1 tbsp	1 tbsp

1 Brush the aubergines with oil, and place under a medium hot grill until they are soft and black.

2 In a bowl, grind together all the remaining ingredients to form a paste.

3 Peel the blackened aubergines and discard the skin.

4 Mash together the aubergine flesh with the spice paste, and serve.

Preparation time 5 minutes.

Cooking time 10 minutes.

CHICK PEA CHUTNEY

This is a refreshing and tangy chutney to serve with any vegetable Balti dish.

SERVES 4–6

INGREDIENTS	METRIC	IMPERIAL	AMERICAN
Chick peas, tinned or cooked	225 g	8 oz	1⅓ cups
Spring onions, coarsely chopped	1 bunch	1 bunch	1 bunch
Lemon juice or vinegar	15 ml	1 tbsp	1 tbsp
Fresh coriander leaves, chopped	15 ml	1 tbsp	1 tbsp
Vegetable oil	15 ml	1 tbsp	1 tbsp
Chilli powder	2.5 ml	½ tsp	½ tsp
Balti Garam Masala	2.5 ml	½ tsp	½ tsp
Salt	to taste	to taste	to taste

1 Mix all the ingredients together.

2 Set aside for 30 minutes.

3 Stir once before serving.

Preparation time 2 minutes.

Standing time 30 minutes.

TOMATO AND ONION CHUTNEY

A tasty alternative to salad, this chutney can be served as a dip with your starters.

SERVES 4–6

INGREDIENTS	METRIC	IMPERIAL	AMERICAN
Onions, finely chopped	3	3	3
Tomatoes, finely sliced	3	3	3
Fresh coriander leaves, chopped	15 ml	1 tbsp	1 tbsp
Mint sauce	5 ml	1 tsp	1 tsp
Lemon or light malt vinegar	7.5 ml	1½ tsp	1½ tsp
Chilli powder	2.5 ml	½ tsp	½ tsp
Balti Garam Masala	2.5 ml	½ tsp	½ tsp
Salt	to taste	to taste	to taste

1 Mix the tomatoes and onions together.

2 Stir in the mint sauce and lemon juice or vinegar.

3 Sprinkle the remaining ingredients over the top of the mixture.

4 Place in the refrigerator for 20–30 minutes. Stir well and serve.

Preparation time 5 minutes.

Chill time 20–30 minutes.

APPLE CHUTNEY

This sweet and sour chutney is a tasty side dish for kebabs. If refrigerated, Apple Chutney will stay fresh for 2–3 weeks.

SERVES 4–6

INGREDIENTS	METRIC	IMPERIAL	AMERICAN
Cooking apples, peeled & cored	450 g	1 lb	1 lb
Seedless raisins	25 g	1 oz	3 tbsp
Fresh green chillies, finely chopped	2	2	2
Vegetable oil	15 ml	1 tbsp	1 tbsp
Fresh ginger, finely chopped	2.5 cm	1 in	1 in
Garlic cloves, finely chopped	3	3	3
Onion seeds	1.5 ml	¼ tsp	¼ tsp
Black cumin seeds	2.5 ml	½ tsp	½ tsp
Ground cumin	10 ml	2 tsp	2 tsp
Salt	to taste	to taste	to taste
Granulated sugar	75 g	3 oz	⅓ cup

1. Finely chop the apples.

2. Heat the oil in a karahi, and fry the onion and cumin seeds for 1 minute.

3. Add the apples, fresh chilli, ginger, garlic and ground cumin. Stir fry for 2–3 minutes.

4. Stir in the sugar and salt. Reduce the heat and cover. Cook for 5 minutes.

5. Add the raisins and stir for 4–5 minutes. The mixture will thicken.

6. Pour into a jar and seal.

Preparation time 5 minutes.

Cooking time 15 minutes.

FRESH CORIANDER CHUTNEY

Hara Dhania Chatni

*T*his *blend of spices and fresh coriander makes a perfect chutney to serve with any Balti. If refrigerated it will keep for up to two weeks.*

SERVES 4

INGREDIENTS	METRIC	IMPERIAL	AMERICAN
Fresh coriander	100 g	4 oz	1 cup
Spring onion, chopped	15 g	½ oz	2 tbsp
Garlic cloves, chopped	2	2	2
Fresh ginger, chopped	1.5 cm	½ in	½ in
Fresh green chillies, seeded	2	2	2
Balti Garam Masala	5 ml	1 tsp	1 tsp
Sugar	5 ml	1 tsp	1 tsp
Salt	to taste	to taste	to taste
Lemon juice	30 ml	2 tbsp	2 tbsp

1 Blend all the ingredients together.

2 Add a little water if the chutney is too stiff.

3 Garnish with slices of fresh lime.

Preparation time 3 minutes.

GREEN MANGO CHUTNEY

*This tart, fruity chutney is the perfect accompani-
ment to any vegetable or lentil Balti. Green Mango
chutney is best eaten on the day that it is made.*

SERVES 4–6

INGREDIENTS	METRIC	IMPERIAL	AMERICAN
Green mango, hard	350 g	12 oz	12 oz
Mango powder	5 ml	1 tsp	1 tsp
Vegetable oil or mustard oil	15 ml	1 tbsp	1 tbsp
Red chillies, dried and crushed	4	4	4
Cumin seeds	4 ml	¾ tsp	¾ tsp
Asafoetida powder	1.5 ml	¼ tsp	¼ tsp
Salt	to taste	to taste	to taste
Fresh coriander, chopped	15 g	½ oz	2 tbsp

1 Grate the mango.

2 Heat the oil over a medium heat. Add the asafoetida powder and the chillies.

3 Fry for 1–2 minutes or until chillies change colour.

4 Add the grated mango, and stir fry for 2 minutes.

5 Stir in the remaining ingredients and mix well.

6 Remove from the heat and leave to cool.

Cooking time 8–10 minutes.

SWEET MANGO CHUTNEY

*T*his sweet chutney is made from ripe mangoes. Simply follow the Green Mango Chutney recipe, replacing green mango with ripe mango and omitting step 4. When you add the mango to the pan, you do not cook it. Simply mix all the ingredients together.

CUCUMBER AND TOMATO RAITA

*I*f you want a tasty side dip for your starters, look no
further. Cucumber and Tomato Raita is a fresh and
crunchy accompaniment for popadoms.

SERVES 4-6

INGREDIENTS	METRIC	IMPERIAL	AMERICAN
Natural yoghurt	200 ml	7 fl oz	1 cup
Mint sauce	5 ml	1 tsp	1 tsp
Fresh coriander leaves, chopped	15 ml	1 tbsp	1 tbsp
Chilli powder	1.5 ml	¼ tsp	¼ tsp
Fresh tomato, chopped	1	1	1
Cucumber, peeled and chopped	7.5 cm	3 in	3 in
Salt	to taste	to taste	to taste

❶ Beat the yoghurt gently with a fork until creamy.

❷ Add the cucumber, tomato, mint and coriander leaves.
Salt to taste. Mix well and chill.

❸ Garnish with a sprig of fresh coriander and sprinkle
with the chilli powder.

Preparation time 5 minutes.

BANANA RAITA

T his gentle, cooling raita is often served with spicy Seekh Kebabs or Balti Madras.

SERVES 4-6

INGREDIENTS	METRIC	IMPERIAL	AMERICAN
Natural yoghurt	200 ml	7 fl oz	1 cup
Cumin seeds	2.5 ml	½ tsp	½ tsp
Onion seeds	2.5 ml	½ tsp	½ tsp
Coriander leaves, chopped	15 ml	1 tbsp	1 tbsp
Banana, sliced	1	1	1

1 Beat the yoghurt gently with a fork until creamy.

2 Heat a frying pan and lightly roast the cumin and onion seeds.

3 Add these to the yoghurt and mix in the remaining ingredients.

4 Chill before serving.

Cooking time 10 minutes.

MINT RAITA

*B*alti addicts will be familiar with this tasty dip as it is
often served with popadoms. You can serve it with
the whole range of starters.

SERVES 4

INGREDIENTS	METRIC	IMPERIAL	AMERICAN
Natural yoghurt	200 ml	7 fl oz	1 cup
Chilli powder	2.5 ml	½ tsp	½ tsp
Balti Garam Masala	2.5 ml	½ tsp	½ tsp
Fresh mint leaves, chopped	15 ml	1 tbsp	1 tbsp
Onion, finely chopped (optional)	15 ml	1 tbsp	1 tbsp

1 Beat the yoghurt gently with a fork until creamy.

2 Stir in the remaining ingredients.

3 Chill before serving.

Preparation time 5 minutes.

CUCUMBER RAITA

This raita combines yoghurt and cucumber in a delicious, cooling side dip to accompany any starter.

SERVES 4

INGREDIENTS	METRIC	IMPERIAL	AMERICAN
Natural yoghurt	200 ml	7 fl oz	1 cup
Cucumber, grated	12.5 cm	5 in	5 in
Fresh green chilli, seeded (optional)	1	1	1
Ground black pepper	5 ml	1 tsp	1 tsp
Fresh coriander leaves, chopped	15 ml	1 tbsp	1 tbsp

1 Finely chop the green chilli.

2 Beat the yoghurt gently with a fork until creamy.

3 Stir in the remaining ingredients.

4 Chill before serving.

Preparation time 5 minutes.

SALAD

There are many different types of salad you can make. Here is a suggested salad recipe that is ideal to serve with Balti starters or main course dishes.

SERVES 4

INGREDIENTS	METRIC	IMPERIAL	AMERICAN
Lettuce	1	1	1
Spanish onion, cut into rings	1	1	1
Carrot, grated	100 g	4 oz	1 cup
Cucumber, cut in triangles	100g	4 oz	1 cup
Fresh tomatoes, quartered	2	2	2
Can sweetcorn, drained	50 g	2 oz	⅓ cup
Salt	5 ml	1 tsp	1 tsp
Pepper, freshly ground	5 ml	1 tsp	1 tsp
Lemon, quartered	1	1	1

1 Mix together the grated carrot, sweetcorn and cucumber.

2 Arrange the lettuce leaves, onion rings and tomatoes on a serving plate. Then place the carrot, sweetcorn and cucumber mixture on to the lettuce leaves.

3 Sprinkle with salt and pepper.

4 Decorate with lemon slices.

SERVING SUGGESTION

For extra flavour, sprinkle with a pinch of chilli powder.

CHAPTER ELEVEN

DESSERTS

Balti sweets are the traditional way to freshen the palette and counteract the spicy nature of main course dishes. A large proportion of Balti desserts are milk and fruit based. Pistachios, cardamom seeds and almonds are often added for flavour and texture.

Many of the sweets are made by reducing milk. This is a long and time-consuming process. Therefore, for the purposes of this quick and easy recipe book, we have included a number of short-cuts using milk powder.

It is worth remembering that you can buy certain Balti desserts, such as Rasmalai, in packet mix form from Asian grocers.

SEMOLINA PUDDING

....

Halwa

*F*lavoured with cardamoms and almonds, this dessert is one of the easiest Halwa desserts to prepare. It is a useful standby for the arrival of unexpected dinner guests.

SERVES 4-6

INGREDIENTS	METRIC	IMPERIAL	AMERICAN
Semolina	175 g	6 oz	1 cup
Granulated sugar	100 g	4 oz	½ cup
Ground cardamom	2.5 ml	½ tsp	½ tsp
Sultanas	25 g	1 oz	2 tbsp
Almonds, blanched and slivered	25 g	1 oz	¼ cup
Milk or water	450 ml	¾ pt	2 cups
Ghee, melted	175 ml	6 fl oz	¾ cup
FOR THE GARNISH			
Flaked almonds	15 ml	1 tbsp	1 tbsp
Sultanas	15 ml	1 tbsp	1 tbsp

❶ In the karahi, lightly roast the semolina until it turns a light brown colour.

❷ Add the ghee and fry for 3-5 minutes until the mixture turns a golden brown.

❸ Turn the heat to low and add the almonds, sultanas, sugar and ground cardamom. Stir fry for 1 minute.

❹ Stir in the milk and leave on a low heat for 1-2 minutes. Stir once and continue cooking for 2-3 minutes or until the mixture thickens.

⑤ Garnish with almonds and sultanas.

SERVING SUGGESTION

Serve hot or cold.

Preparation time 5 minutes.

Cooking time 15 minutes.

GULAB JAMAN

T hese golden-brown sponge balls are steeped in a subtly flavoured syrup. They can be served hot or cold.

SERVES 4–6

INGREDIENTS	METRIC	IMPERIAL	AMERICAN
FOR THE SPONGE BALLS			
Milk powder	175 g	6 oz	1½ cups
Self-raising flour	40 g	1½ oz	⅓ cup
Melted butter or ghee	40 g	1½ oz	3 tbsp
Ground cardamom	2.5 ml	½ tsp	½ tsp
Milk	85 ml	3 fl oz	5½ tbsp
Cooking oil	350 ml	12 fl oz	1½ cups
FOR THE SYRUP			
Granulated sugar	225 g	8 oz	1 cup
Ground cardamom	2.5 ml	½ tsp	½ tsp
Water	600 ml	1 pt	2½ cups
Rose water (optional)	7.5 ml	1½ tsp	1½ tsp

❶ Place all the syrup ingredients in a saucepan. Bring to the boil, then lower the heat and simmer for 20 minutes without stirring.

❷ In a bowl, add the milk powder, flour and ground cardamom. Stir in the melted butter and gradually add the milk to form a soft dough.

❸ Divide the dough into 15–16 equal parts and roll into balls.

④ Cook for 4–5 minutes until they are a deep golden brown.

⑤ Remove them from the pan and drain them on absorbent kitchen paper. Allow to cool for 5 minutes.

⑥ Place the Gulab Jamans into a bowl and pour on the syrup. Sprinkle with rose water and leave for 15 minutes before serving.

SERVING SUGGESTION

Gulab Jamans can be eaten warm or cold. Add a dash of brandy for that extra special occasion.

Preparation time 20 minutes.

Cooking time 20 minutes.

SEMOLINA AND ALMOND HALWA

T his is a fudge-like sweetmeat to serve with coffee after dinner. It also makes a delicious dessert.

SERVES 6–8

INGREDIENTS	METRIC	IMPERIAL	AMERICAN
Ghee	175 g	6 oz	¾ cup
Semolina	175 g	6 oz	1 cup
Ground almonds	175 g	6 oz	1½ cups
Ground nutmeg	2.5 ml	½ tsp	½ tsp
Ground cardamom	2.5 ml	½ tsp	½ tsp
Can condensed milk, sweetened	400 g	14 oz	1¼ cup
FOR THE GARNISH			
Flaked almonds	15 ml	1 tbsp	1 tbsp

1. Grease a shallow baking tray.

2. Melt the ghee in a pan and add the semolina. Stirring continuously, cook for 4–6 minutes or until the mixture is golden brown.

3. Remove from the heat. Add the spices and almonds, and mix thoroughly.

4. Pour in the milk gradually until a smooth paste is formed.

5. Return to the heat and stir continuously until the mixture has thickened.

6. Pour into the greased tray and leave to cool.

7. Garnish with flaked almonds and cut into squares to serve.

Cooking time 10–15 minutes.

RASMALAI

*R*asmalai *is made by reducing milk to a solid 'khoya', and then flavouring it with pistachio, cardamom and almond. This means that it is very time-consuming to make. However, with one or two short-cuts, you can cook a delicious Rasmalai at home. Alternatively, you can buy Rasmalai in packet mix form from Asian grocers.*

SERVES 4–6

INGREDIENTS	METRIC	IMPERIAL	AMERICAN
Full cream milk powder	175 g	6 oz	1½ cups
Baking powder	5 ml	1 tsp	1 tsp
Melted ghee	2.5 ml	½ tsp	½ tsp
Egg, beaten	1	1	1
Pistachio, roughly chopped	30 ml	2 tbsp	2 tbsp
Milk	600 ml	1 pt	2½ cups
Sugar	100 g	4 oz	½ cup

1 Mix together the milk powder and baking powder, and gradually stir in the beaten egg to form a firm, soft dough. If it is too dry, add some melted ghee.

2 Mould the dough into small sausage shapes.

3 In a pan, heat the milk and sugar, and bring to the boil.

4 Add the milk sausages, and simmer on low heat for 2–3 minutes. The milk sausages will expand.

5 Pour into a dish and sprinkle with the pistachio.

6 Serve chilled.

Preparation time 15 minutes.

Cooking time 5 minutes.

ALMOND ICED DESSERT

Badam Ki Kulfi

*O*ften referred to as 'Indian ice cream', this is a rich and creamy iced dessert, made with full cream milk and almonds, and sometimes flavoured with rose water. We have used evaporated milk here to avoid the time-consuming process of reducing milk.

SERVES 6-8

INGREDIENTS	METRIC	IMPERIAL	AMERICAN
Evaporated milk	600 ml	1 pt	2½ cups
Single cream	300 ml	½ pt	1¼ cups
Granulated sugar	100 g	4 oz	½ cup
Ground almonds	25 g	1 oz	¼ cup
Almond essence	2.5 ml	½ tsp	½ tsp
FOR THE GARNISH			
Pistachio, unsalted and shelled	15 ml	1 tbsp	1 tbsp

1. Place all the ingredients, except the almond essence, in a pan.

2. Bring to the boil, stirring frequently.

3. Reduce the heat and simmer for 5-6 minutes, stirring constantly.

4. Remove from the heat and allow to cool, stirring the mixture frequently so a skin does not form.

5. When cooled, pour in the almond essence.

6. Pour the mixture into ice cream moulds and freeze for 4-6 hours.

⑦ Leave at room temperature for 5 minutes before removing from the mould.

⑧ Sprinkle with lightly chopped pistachios.

SERVING SUGGESTION

Serve with fruit purée.

Preparation time 5 minutes.

Cooking time 12–15 minutes.

Freezing time 4–6 hours.

JALABIS

Grown extensively throughout Kashmir, saffron combines beautifully with rose water in this mouth-watering recipe.

SERVES 4-6

INGREDIENTS	METRIC	IMPERIAL	AMERICAN
Plain white flour	275 g	10 oz	2½ cups
Baking powder	7.5 ml	1½ tsp	1½ tsp
Strands of saffron, ground	8	8	8
Water, boiling	30 ml	2 tbsp	2 tbsp
Water, warm	300 ml	½ pt	1¼ cups
Sugar	275 g	10 oz	1¼ cups
Rose water	7.5 ml	1½ tsp	1½ tsp
Oil for deep frying	375 ml	13 fl oz	1½ cups

1 Sift the flour and baking powder into a bowl.

2 Add enough warm water to form the batter mixture which should have a 'pouring' consistency.

3 Soak the saffron in the boiling water, then mash it and strain off the yellow liquid into the batter mix.

4 Heat the oil, without burning it.

5 Pipe the batter through a small funnel into curled shapes, each about 5 cm/2 inches across, on to the oil. Cook on both sides until crisp and golden.

6 Remove the jalabis with a serrated spoon.

7 Make a syrup by boiling the sugar and remaining water together for 8 minutes. Flavour with the rose water and pour over the jalabis.

8 Set aside for 30 minutes before serving.

Preparation time 10 minutes.
Cooking time 10 minutes.

CHAPTER TWELVE

DRINKS

If you want to enjoy the authentic Balti experience, you should serve traditional drinks with your Balti meal. These refreshing drinks will cleanse and freshen the palette, without overpowering the flavours of your meal.

If you prefer a little alcohol, we would recommend a traditional Indian lager, served chilled. Brewed in India, these lagers will complement any Balti dish.

To finish your meal in style, serve cardamom flavoured coffee and a delicious sweetmeat instead of the usual chocolate mints.

LASSI

This is a frothy, chilled yoghurt drink that has either a sweet or a salty flavour. You can add chopped or puréed fresh summer fruits to your favourite Lassi for extra flavour.

SWEET LASSI

MAKES 1 pint

INGREDIENTS	METRIC	IMPERIAL	AMERICAN
Natural yoghurt	300 ml	½ pt	1¼ cups
Sugar	5 ml	1 tsp	1 tsp
Water, cold	300 ml	½ pt	1¼ cups
Crushed ice cubes	to taste	to taste	to taste
FOR THE GARNISH			
Fresh mint leaves	5 ml	1 tsp	1 tsp

1 Whisk together all the ingredients.

2 Add the crushed ice and garnish with mint leaves.

NOTE:

For extra creamy Lassi, replace the water with milk.

SALT LASSI

*T*his delicious Lassi variation is ideal for those hot summer months.

MAKES 1 pint

INGREDIENTS	METRIC	IMPERIAL	AMERICAN
Natural yoghurt	300 ml	½ pt	1¼ cups
Water, cold	300 ml	½ pt	1¼ cups
Salt	2.5 ml	½ tsp	½ tsp
Crushed ice cubes	to taste	to taste	to taste

1 Whisk together all the ingredients.

2 Add crushed ice and serve.

Almond Cocktail Concentrate

*A lmonds grow profusely in the lush valleys of Balti-
stan and Kashmir. They are often used for flavouring sweets and drinks. This cocktail is a traditional
sweet concentrate that you mix with milk. You can
store it in a refrigerator for up to six weeks.*

MAKES 1.2 litres / 2 pints

INGREDIENTS	METRIC	IMPERIAL	AMERICAN
Almonds, shelled	450 g	1 lb	4 cups
Sugar	450 g	1 lb	2 cups
Water	950 ml	1⅔ pt	4 cups
Cardamom seeds	2.5 ml	½ tsp	½ tsp
Milk	450 ml	¾ pt	2 cups

1 Grind together the almonds and cardamom seeds.

2 Place the sugar and water in a pan, add the blended almonds, and heat until the sauce thickens.

3 Allow to cool, then add 1 tbsp of this concentrate mixture to hot or cold milk.

4 Whisk and serve.

SERVING SUGGESTION

Serve either hot or cold.

Preparation time 5 minutes.

Cooking time 7 minutes.

AROMATIC FRUIT JUICE

*I*t is quick and easy to enrich your favourite fruit juice - for example, orange, pineapple or apple juice - with exotic flavoured spices.

SERVES 4

INGREDIENTS	METRIC	IMPERIAL	AMERICAN
Fruit juice	600 ml	1 pt	2½ cups
Whole green cardamoms, tops pinched	3-4	3-4	3-4
Whole clove	1	1	1
Cassia bark	2.5 cm	1 in	1 in
Lemon juice	30 ml	2 tbsp	2 tbsp
FOR THE GARNISH			
Segmented orange or lemon	1	1	1

1 Pour the fruit juice into a pan.

2 Add the spices and heat gently for 5 minutes. Do not boil.

3 Remove from the heat and pour in the lemon juice.

4 Allow to cool before garnishing with orange or lemon.

Preparation time 5 minutes.

CARDAMOM COFFEE

Illachi Coffee

This is an unusual way to serve your coffee after dinner. For an extra treat, serve it with grated chocolate sprinkled on top.

SERVES 4-6

INGREDIENTS	METRIC	IMPERIAL	AMERICAN
Ground cardamom	7.5 ml	1½ tsp	1½ tsp
Ground coffee of your choice	50 g	2 oz	½ cup
Water	600 ml	1 pt	2½ cups
TO SERVE			
Cream	to taste	to taste	to taste
Sugar	to taste	to taste	to taste

1. Mix together the coffee and ground cardamom.

2. Now make the coffee in a cafetière or filter, as you would normally.

3. Serve hot with cream and sugar to taste.

Preparation time 15 minutes.

NOTE:

If you normally use instant coffee, replace the ground cardamom with 5-6 whole green cardamoms. Boil the water and whole cardamoms together, then remove the cardamoms and make your coffee as normal.

CHAPTER THIRTEEN

MENU
IDEAS

Balti makes a great meal, whatever the occasion - from a simple family gathering to a more elaborate business meal. Here are some interesting menu ideas.

FAMILY MEAL

This is a nutritious and delightful Balti menu for all the family. Children will particularly enjoy the crispy popadoms and the sweet jalabis.

STARTERS

Popadoms

Vegetable Samosa

Mint Raita

Tamarind and Onion Chutney

MAIN COURSE

Chicken Balti

Potato Balti

Sweet Mango Chutney

Chapati

SWEET

Jalabis

DRINKS

Almond Cocktail

Fruit Juice

Chilled water

FUN MENU

*I*f you have invited friends over for a fun evening,
you can choose Balti dishes that bring colour and
excitement to the table.

STARTERS

Spicy Lamb Chops
Chicken Tikka
Salad

MAIN DISHES

Orange and Chicken Balti
Prawn, Potato and Spinach Balti
Mixed Vegetable Balti
Cucumber Raita
Fresh Coriander Chutney
Chapati

SWEET

Gulab Jaman
Kulfi

DRINKS

Indian Lager
Sweet Lassi
Chilled water
Illachi Coffee
Semolina and Almond Halwa

UPMARKET MENU

I mportant dinner parties can be a nightmare, especially if you are keen to impress your boss or prospective customers. Why not choose a range of aromatically spiced Balti dishes that will delight your guests without overpowering them?

STARTERS

Popadoms
Meat Samosa
Mixed Vegetable Pakora
Onion Bhaji
Mint Raita
Tamarind and Onion Chutney

MAIN COURSE

Balti Butter Chicken
Balti Lamb Rogan Josh
Mogul King Prawn Balti
Aubergine (Eggplant) Balti
Mushroom Balti
Naan Bread
Boiled Rice

SWEETS

Rasmalai
Kulfi

DRINKS

Lassi, sweet or salty
Fruit juice
Chilled water
Illachi Coffee
Semolina and Almond Halwa

AL FRESCO

When summer has arrived and you have brushed away the cobwebs from the barbecue, why not celebrate with a simple Balti barbecue?

STARTERS

Seekh Kebabs

Tandoori Fish

Salad

Aubergine (Eggplant) Chutney

Banana Raita

MAIN COURSE

Beef Balti

Chicken Tikka Masala

   (warm the Masala sauce and pour it over the freshly
   barbecued tikka)

Okra Dopiaza

Chapati

SWEET

Kulfi

DRINKS

Sweet Lassi

   (add chopped strawberries or sweet mango)

CHAPTER FOURTEEN

STOCKING YOUR PANTRY

Apart from the perishable items mentioned in this book, all of the utensils and spices - including the special Balti Masala blends - are available from the Birmingham Balti Co., 308 Telsen Centre, 55 Thomas Street, Aston, Birmingham B6 4TN. Telephone or fax on 0121 359 8388 for a brochure and details of your local stockist.

Available from the Birmingham Balti Co.

SPICES

MASALA BLENDS

Balti Masala
Balti Garam Masala
Tandoori Masala

WHOLE SPICES

Aniseed seeds
Bay leaves
Cardamoms, whole green
Cardamoms, whole black
Cardamom seeds
Cassia bark
Chillies, dried red
Cloves, whole
Coriander seeds
Cumin seeds, black
Cumin seeds, white
Curry leaves
Fennel seeds
Fenugreek leaves, dried
Fenugreek seeds
Lovage seeds
Mint leaves, dried
Mustard seeds
Onion seeds

GROUND SPICES

Asafoetida powder
Aniseed
Cardamom
Chilli
Cloves
Coriander
Cumin

Fenugreek
Garlic powder
Ginger
Fennel
Mango powder
Paprika
Turmeric
Tamarind block

FOODSTUFFS

Basmati rice
Chapati flour - available in light wholemeal or brown
    wholemeal
Popadoms - available in five flavours: garlic, cumin, black
    pepper, red chilli or plain
Rasmalai dessert mix

UTENSILS

Karahi - made from wrought iron and mild steel, in various
    sizes, suitable for any cooking medium
Kadoi - stainless steel serving pan, in various sizes
Masala Dabba - made from stainless steel, double lidded for
    freshness, in various sizes
Tawa - in one size, for cooking perfect chapatis

The Birmingham Balti Co. also offers three styles of Balti
    Cookery Kits - the ideal introduction to Balti cuisine.

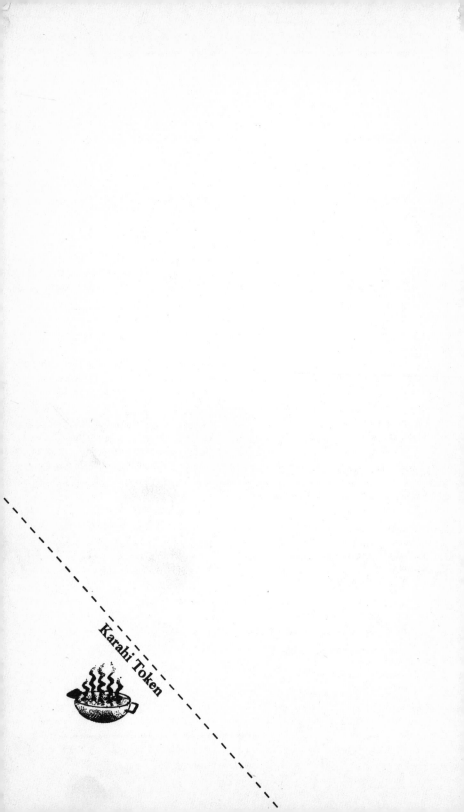

Karahi Token